THE DILEMMA
OF THE TALENTED HEROINE

A study in Nineteenth Century fiction

Susan Siefert

EDEN PRESS

Monographs in
Women's Studies

Series Editor:
Sherri Clarkson

THE DILEMMA
OF THE TALENTED HEROINE

A study in Nineteenth Century fiction

Susan Siefert

© Eden Press Inc. 1977

Published in 1978 by

Eden Press Inc.
1538 Sherbrooke St. West, #201
Montreal, Quebec, Canada
H3G 1L5

and

Eden Medical Research Inc.
Box 51
St. Albans, Vermont 05478
U.S.A.

ISBN 0-88831-018-8

Printed in Great Britain by A. Wheaton & Co. Ltd. Exeter.

PREFACE

The nineteenth century woman and the heroines of the nineteenth century novel are frequently conceived of in stereotyped terms. All too often these women are regarded, without exception, as creatures who were kind, gentle, unaspiring, unassertive, and intellectually feeble. This study explores the limitations of this stereotype by focusing upon five a-typical heroines of nineteenth century fiction: Elizabeth Bennet of *Pride and Prejudice*, Emma Woodhouse of *Emma*, Dorothea Brooke of *Middlemarch*, Maggie Tulliver of *The Mill on the Floss*, and Charlotte Bronte's Jane Eyre. Each of these heroines possesses that combination of moral sensitivity, intellectual acuity and aspiration which comprises "talent." Each heroine is confronted with this dilemma: How does one reconcile personal aspirations with the demands of a society which is distinctly uncongenial to such aspirations? This study examines the reasons for each heroine's ultimate success or failure as she attempts this reconciliation, in terms of self-image, the self and society, self-definition, aspiration and limitation, and the integration of the self and society. This study does not attempt to provide a new interpretation of each of the five novels. Rather, it is hoped that its chief contribution will be to provide a different way of looking at the nineteenth century heroine through the consistent application of the particular perspective afforded by the concept of "talent."

Susan Siefert
1977

ACKNOWLEDGMENTS

I am grateful to the American Association of University Women for a generous research fellowship which provided welcome support during the preparation of this book. My task was considerably facilitated by the competent and amiable assistance which I received from the respective staffs of the Marquette University Memorial Library, the Milwaukee Public Library, the Research Center for Women at Alverno College, the University of Wisconsin Library and the New York Public Library.

Equally valuable were the useful criticisms and timely suggestions afforded by my colleagues in the Department of English at Marquette University. Special thanks is owed to two members in particular, Professors Jerome Thale and M. Paton Ryan.

In the editing and preparation of this manuscript for publication, I was especially fortunate to have the counsel and assistance of close and valued friends, Joseph F. Marcey, Jr. of The Viking Press, Cheryl Marshall, and Jane B. and Thomas E. Hachey.

TABLE OF CONTENTS

TO MY FATHER AND MOTHER:
ROBERT AND ROSEMARY SIEFERT

Chapter 1

THE PROBLEM OF STEREOTYPE
AND THE DILEMMA OF TALENT

*...if there were one level of feminine incompetence as strict
as the ability to count three and no more, the social lot of
women might be treated with scientific certitude. Meanwhile
the indefiniteness remains and the limits of variation are
really much wider than one would imagine from the sameness of women's coiffure and the favourite love stories in
prose and verse.*[1]

In this passage from the *Prelude* to *Middlemarch* George Eliot focuses upon
three themes which are of major importance in a consideration of the status
of women in nineteenth century life and fiction. The condition of being
female is somehow associated with a degree of incompetence, inadequacy
and ineffectuality. Allied to this is the notion that the area in which women's
"incompetence" appears most markedly is the social: the sphere in which she
relates, or attempts to relate, to other human beings. There is an implied
recognition that a prevailing stereotype of women exists and that the stereotype is both superficial and untrue. Despite the "sameness of women's coiffure" and their standardized portrayal in popular literature, there is a wide
area of indefiniteness, of incertitude and variation and, Eliot implies, this area
which defies "scientific certitude" is a potentially meaningful and intriguing one.

In her recognition of the existence of a stereotyped view of women, Eliot calls
attention to the historical reality of the strong and pervasive codes for women

1

to which the society of nineteenth century Britain exacted homage and to the set of expectations which society had evolved for women. Numerous studies have been devoted to the detailed examination of social expectations for women and to the degree to which the nineteenth century women, in fact and fiction, conformed to them.[2] These studies generally agree that the novels of the nineteenth century portray woman's role and society's expectations of her with fidelity and historical accuracy. An attempt to reiterate what the investigations of these scholars have already demonstrated would be superfluous, but it is useful to review, in summary, some of their findings.

FEMININE STEREOTYPES

The nineteenth century expected women to possess a delicacy of form and feature with an accompanying deficiency in physical prowess. A lack of intellectual ability was viewed as the natural and becoming corollary to physical delicacy. The virtues required of the middle-class young lady were chiefly gentleness, tenderness, and consideration for others, while the imperfections permitted her included impulsiveness, flightiness, an absorption in the trivial, and an incapacity for friendship with other women.[3] This last defect was assumed to be a natural by-product of jealousy, for the function of the nineteenth century girl was courtship and marriage. Marriage was a competition of the keenest sort[4] and true friendship with other competitors was clearly considered impossible and imprudent.

One writer describes the young lady's preparation for marriage this way:

> To get ready for the marriage market a girl was trained like a race-horse. Her education consisted of showy accomplishments designed to ensnare young men. The three R's of this deadly equipment were music, drawing, and French, administered by a governess at home . . . or, by mistresses in an inferior boarding school. Miss Pinkerton's academy described in Vanity Fair was probably typical of the more ambitious girls' school.[5]

When one recalls that Amelia Sedley emerged from six years' residence at Chiswick Mall with the following accomplishments, one can only wonder at the superficiality which must have distinguished the graduates of the less "ambitious" girls' schools:

2

> *In music, in dancing, in orthography, in every variety of embroidery and needle-work, she will be found to have realised her friends' fondest wishes . In geography there is still much to be desired; and a careful and undeviating use of the backboard for four hours daily during the next three years, is recommended as necessary to the acquirement of that dignified deportment and carriage, so requisite for every young lady of fashion.[6]*

The popular ideal of women is best revealed in Dr. Gregory's *Legacy to My Daughters* (1774) which was acclaimed with such enthusiasm that it was reprinted at intervals throughout the next hundred years.[7] Dr. Gregory's strictures have been succinctly summarized by scholars as enjoining upon women the virtues of long-suffering, humility, modesty, chastity and the necessity to suppress any evidences of wit, good sense and learning.[8] It is, however, instructive to sample a few passages of Dr. Gregory's prose; the highly negative nature of his "legacy" is perhaps most clearly revealed when one notes the rhetorical emphasis upon dissimulation and the high premium placed upon feminine unnaturalness. With regard to intelligence, Dr. Gregory warns:

> *Wit is the most dangerous talent you possess. It must be guarded with great discretion and good nature, otherwise it will create you many enemies . . . Be even cautious in displaying your good sense. It will be thought you assume a superiority over the rest of the company. But if you happen to have any learning, keep it a profound secret, especially from the men, who generally look with a jealous and malignant eye on a woman of great parts, and a cultivated understanding . . .[9]*

The same secretive, almost surreptitious, tone marks Dr. Gregory's remarks on good health:

> *But although good health be one of the greatest blessings of life, never make a boast of it, but enjoy it in grateful silence. We so naturally associate the idea of female softness and delicacy with a correspondent delicacy of constitution, that when a woman speaks of her great strength, her extraordinary appetite, her ability to bear excessive fatigue, we*

3

recoil at the description in a way she is little aware of.[10]

Dr. Gregory frankly advises his readers of the necessity of role-playing for social survival:

> *The power of a fine woman over the hearts of men, of men*
> *of the finest parts, is even beyond what she conceives. They*
> *are sensible of the pleasing illusion, but they cannot, nor do*
> *they wish to dissolve it. But if she is determined to dispel*
> *the charm, it certainly is in her power, she may soon reduce*
> *the angel to a very ordinary girl.*[11]

The fear that the "angel" might be reduced to "a very ordinary girl" was a very real one; for upon this conception of woman as angel rested the stability of the middle and upper classes's concept of love, marriage, and home life.[12] The standards of artificiality, self-repression and exaggerated sweetness were not relaxed after marriage. Once her goal was attained, the "shy" maiden assumed the even more uncomfortable and precarious pedestal of the "angel in the house." A sample of even one sonnet from Coventry Patmore's immensely popular sonnet sequence reveals many of the assumptions underlying the characterization of woman as essentially angelic in nature. The "Married Lover" asks:

> *Why, having won her, do I woo?*
> *Because her spirit's vestal grace*
> *Provokes me always to pursue,*
> *But, spirit-like, eludes embrace;*
> *Because her womanhood is such*
> *That, as on court-days subjects kiss*
> *The Queen's hand, yet so near a touch*
> *Affirms no mean familiarness, . . .*[13]

One of the chief paradoxes of *The Angel in the House* lies in the very title: the woman is conceived of as ethereal, scarcely mortal, yet she is relegated to the temporal environs of "the house." In the portion of "The Married Lover" quoted above, this ideal of the woman as scarcely possessing a physical dimension is elaborated. The lover speaks primarily of her spirit to which he attaches the adjective "vestal," a word since Roman times associated with virginity. This application of a virginal attribute to a married woman is not as puzzling as it may at first appear. The total effect achieved is the negation of

4

the wife's physicality and sexuality; the integrity of her existence as a human being is nullified, to be replaced with an illusory "elevation" to the realm of a purely spiritual existence. When the speaker of the poem does consider his wife's "womanhood" he effects the same kind of negation by comparing their marital embraces to the artificial, ceremonial kiss which the obedient subject chastely bestows upon the Queen's hand.

The application of angelic attributes to women was not unique to Patmore's writing. In Tennyson's *The Princess*, the Prince describes his mother as "No angel, but a dearer being, all dipt / In angel instincts, breathing Paradise . . ."[14] Perhaps nothing more clearly illustrates the denial of woman's full humanity as a sexual being than the recognition that the "Married Lover" addresses his wife in terms as chaste, ethereal and idealized as those employed by the Prince in praising his mother.

ALTERNATIVES TO THE STEREOTYPES

A discordant but refreshing note is introduced by a consideration of Mary Wollstonecraft's rather acid assessment, written over fifty years before *The Princess* appeared, of the essential incongruity involved in elevating woman to an angelic status while simultaneously maintaining her in an intellectually servile position:

> *Into what inconsistencies do men fall when they argue without the compass of principles. Women, weak women, are compared with angels; yet, a superior order of beings should be supposed to possess more intellect than man; or in what does their superiority consist? In the same strain, to drop the sneer, they are allowed to possess more goodness of heart, piety, and benevolence. I doubt the fact . . . unless ignorance be allowed to be the mother of devotion; for I am firmly persuaded that, on the average, the proportion between virtue and knowledge is more upon a par than is commonly granted.*[15]

Mary Wollstonecraft was denying the equation, popular in the eighteenth century and honored as dogma in the nineteenth, of ignorance with innocence, of virtue with mindless submission. But hers was truly a voice crying in the wilderness. After the upheavals in France, with cries for rights ending in

5

bloodshed and tyranny, few Englishmen wished to engage in controversy over a book whose very title rendered it suspect. Indeed, "virtuous" women, like Hannah More, prided themselves upon never having read the book while they soundly condemned its author. But Mary Wolstonecraft's ideas were harbingers of things to come and *A Vindication of the Rights of Woman* is one illustration of a phenomenon that has yet to receive sufficient attention or study. While much effort has been expended in delineating the nature of the stereotype of women which prevailed in the nineteenth century, comparatively little note has been taken of the fact that gifted thinkers in the nineteenth century and before, as well as novelists like Jane Austen, Charlotte Bronte and George Eliot, were aware of the limited truth of the stereotype and were concerned with presenting viable alternatives to Thackeray's "Amelia doll"-- the heroine who was kind, gentle, unassertive, unaspiring and intellectually moribund. Matthew Arnold and George Eliot, for instance, wrote in their essays and novels, respectively, about the dilemma of the a-typical woman: the woman possessed of heroic aspirations in an unheroic age. Indeed, so critical did the dilemma of the aspiring but frustrated woman appear to Eliot and Arnold that each invoked the rhetorical motif of the "saint" in considering this dilemma.

In the *Prelude* to *Middlemarch*, George Eliot's heroine, Dorothea, is contrasted with the great St. Theresa of Avila whose "passionate ideal nature demanded an epic life" and who found her own personal fulfillment in an age when heroism was still possible. *Middlemarch*, however, is subtitled "A Study of Provincial Life" and Dorothea is a "later-born Theresa . . . helped by no coherent social faith and order which could perform the function of knowledge for the ardently willing soul." (*M*, 3) Similarly, Arnold in his "Eugenie de Guerin" essay considers this woman of "clearness and firmness of intelligence"[16] in terms of the saint. Eugenie, however, is not an "ideal saint"; she is not "one of those saints arrived at perfect sweetness and calm, steeped in ecstasy; there is something primitive, indomitable in her . . ."[17] Like Eliot, Arnold was interested in the quality of his heroine's struggle: an aspiring character in an age distinctly uncongenial to such aspiration, she had always to contend with "a certain *ennui* which I have in me."[18]

THE TALENTED HEROINE

This struggle with *ennui*, discontent and boredom arising from the tension between individual aspiration and an uncongenial society distinguishes five of the most engaging heroines of nineteenth century fiction: Jane Austen's Elizabeth Bennet and Emma Woodhouse, Charlotte Bronte's Jane Eyre, and George Eliot's Maggie Tulliver and Dorothea Brooke. These heroines are intriguing because they dwell in that area of "indefiniteness" of which George Eliot wrote and, among them, they exhibit those wide "limits of variation" which compelled Eliot's interest.

One factor which places these five heroines within Eliot's category of "indefiniteness" is their respective positions vis a vis the expectations of their societies. None of these heroines exhibits an extreme or uncompromising stance with relation to her social world. While each of them dwells in a society which has stereotyped expectations for young ladies, no one heroine aspires to or is capable of completely fulfilling these social demands. In short, we do not find an Amelia Sedley among them. Neither, however, do we encounter a Becky Sharp. While Amelia represents one extreme in her absolute fidelity to convention, Becky is a kind of anti-heroine, whose goals and interests not only conflict with societal expectations but whose motives, from the moment when she hurls "Johnson's Dixonary" from the coach, are directly subversive to the social order. While Becky is certainly a more compelling character than Amelia, she too represents an extreme and, hence, an absolute. There is nothing "indefinite" about Becky's character, any more than there is about the character of Catherine Earnshaw of *Wuthering Heights*. Catherine neither conforms to, nor subverts, society because she is located in the world of romance where life is a complicated but not complex matter of self-assertion.

The characters of Elizabeth, Emma, Jane, Maggie and Dorothea interest us because they are complex: they seek to attain a poise or an acceptable compromise between their individual aspirations and societal expectations. The search for this poise involves growth, variety and a kind of "negative capability" to deal with indefiniteness. Although the conventions which frustrate these heroines are nineteenth century ones, the problem of the conflicting claims of society and the individual need for self-assertion and self-fulfillment is a timeless and a universal one.

The conventions with which the aspirations of these five heroines conflict may sometimes appear to be superficial. Conventions, customs, and societal expectations are, however, evolved by human beings and, however obliquely, they are retained because they fulfill such human needs as self-definition, security and a sense of community. Just as the superficially sentimental and gratuitous characterization of women as angelic can be pressed to reveal a society's fear of, and ambivalence towards, female sexuality, so Elizabeth Bennet's energetic walk in the mud[19] not only reveals her to be no devotee of Dr. Gregory, but immediately sets her at odds, by virtue of her energy, with the fashionable languor of her society. The narrator in *Middlemarch* remarks, "Women were expected to have weak opinions; but the great safeguard of society and of domestic life was, that opinions were not acted on." (*M*, 7) This information establishes society's need for an intellectual deficiency in women and implies strongly that the individual who defies this convention risks the defensive retribution of society. In light of this sentence such stereotyped judgments as Mr. Brooke's "Young ladies don't understand political economy, you know" (*M*, 12) and "Young ladies are too flighty" (*M*, 14) carry an ominous comment upon Dorothea's budding intellectual ardor. Lydgate's apparently superficial and conventional admiration of Rosamund, "She is grace itself; she is perfectly lovely and accomplished. That is what a woman ought to be: she ought to produce the effect of exquisite music.", ironically predicts his own future loss of aspiration and capitulation to society's demands for himself (*M*, 69-70). When Mr. Tulliver ruefully remarks Maggie's intellectual ability and assesses her worth in terms of her potential value in the marriage market—"It's no mischief when she's a little un, but an over-'cute woman's no better than a long-tailed sheep--She'll fetch none the better price for that,"[20] he not only establishes the vulgar, mercantile nature of St. Ogg society, but hints at the evolution of Maggie's tragedy from the conflict between her acuity and her society's practical rigidity.

Just as conventions and stereotyped notions are, in these novels, more significant for the heroines' futures than they may at first appear, so too, seemingly conventional people figure importantly in the search for self-fulfillment of the five heroines under consideration. The conventionality of such female characters as Jane Bennet, Isabella Knightley, Celia Brooke and Lucy Deane often serves to foil and display the unconventional attributes of the talented heroines. Other minor female characters such as Charlotte Lucas, Jane Fairfax, Rosamund Vincy and Georgiana and Eliza Reed pose various kinds of frustrations to the sensibilities and aspirations of the five talented heroines: Elizabeth Bennet, Emma Woodhouse, Dorothea Brooke, Maggie Tulliver and Jane Eyre. The secondary female characters deserve our attention because they not only illustrate how the talented heroines depart from stereotyped patterns, but also because they frequently serve the critical function of exposing the follies and illusions of the talented heroines.

It is difficult to generalize freely about such a large number of subordinate, but important, characters; but it can be observed that most of the conventional females in the five novels are characterized as "accomplished." That is, they can play and sing, sketch, paint, do fancy needlework, and play the conventional role expected of the young lady in her relationships with the opposite sex. Rosamund Vincy in *Middlemarch* represents the absolute paragon of accomplishment, "She was admitted to be the flower of Mrs. Lemon's school," (*M*, 71) but all of the conventional female characters are accomplished to some degree.

The five heroines of the novels, however, are distinguished from the norm by their lack of accomplishments, either through disinterest, inablitiy, or a lack of self-discipline. Elizabeth Bennet cannot play "half so well" as her accomplished sister Mary (*P & P*, 17); Emma Woodhouse lacks the "steadiness" and self-discipline to excel in drawing and music[21]; Jane Eyre has the traditional accomplishments of the governess, but to Rochester's critical ear her piano playing is "like any other English schoolgirl"[22]; unlike her accomplished cousin Lucy, Maggie Tulliver "can do nothing more difficult or more elegant than shirt-making" (*MF*, 330); Dorothea Brooke's intellectual ardor precludes any interest in the frivolous or the aesthetic--even horseback riding causes guilt feelings (*M*, 13) and art confuses and affronts her Puritanical sympathies (*M*, 143).[23]

The heroines' lack of accomplishments functions in the five novels in a number of ways. Most obviously, this deficiency distinguishes the heroines from the conventional--and sometimes superficial--women. Because society expects a young girl to possess certain skills, the heroines' failure in this respect represents and sometimes underscores their alienation from society. But the heroines' lack of accomplishment also works positively to accentuate what they do have: a combination of intellectual acuity, moral sensitivity and aspiration which shall be designated as "talent." As distinct from accomplishment, talent is an interior quality, intimately related to the heroines' self-images and the possession of this quality involves the talented heroine in a complex dilemma. Because of her intellectual acuity, she often sees more and more deeply than others do; sometimes she perceives meanings which elude the conventional women, sometimes her world view is so different that she misses what is perfectly apparent to others. Her moral sensitivity is most often a source of pain to her; it gives her a sense of perception almost as keen as "hearing the grass grow and the squirrel's heart beat"--she does not have the "wadding of stupidity" (*M*, 144) which protects the more conventional individual. About her sense of aspiration it is difficult to generalize. Each of the talented heroines has a unique set of ambitions. But to a greater or lesser degree, her aspiration involves both a conflict within herself and with the prevailing mores of her society.

All this is not to say that the five talented heroines are perfect. They are dynamic characters who grow, during the course of their novels, to realize their talent as fully as each of them can. Elizabeth Bennet possesses intellectual refinement and moral sensitivity from the first; her task is to discover these latent qualities. Emma Woodhouse, by contrast, possesses a keen but unrefined intellect; she must be painfully educated into moral sensitivity. Dorothea Brooke is given to extremes; she must learn both to channel and to tone the quality of her aspiration if she is to exert any influence at all upon provincial life.

Nor is this category of talent meant to suggest that the conventional women characters in the novels are necessarily immoral, insensitive or complacent. Rosamund Vincy certainly has aspirations, Lucy Deane is one of the most morally sensitive characters in all of the novels, and Jane Fairfax has a subtle and complex intellect whose workings confound even the quick-witted Emma. None of the conventional women, however, has the precise combination of qualities which distinguishes the talented heroine. Because they lack one or more of these characteristics, the accomplished women often act as foil characters to the virtues of the talented heroine. This, however, is frequently a secondary function. A close examination of each heroine's relationship with the conventional women who inhabit her world reveals that each of them, to some degree, is a source of conflict for the talented heroine and each elicits some different facet of the "dilemma of talent."

THE TALENTED HEROINE AND THE CONVENTIONAL WOMAN

Elizabeth Bennet's relationship with her sister Jane is illustrative of the kinds of conflict which intellectual acuity can pose for the talented woman. Elizabeth is a witty, self-assertive, highly critical woman. She enjoys distancing herself from her society and is amused by the ironic contemplation of the follies of others: "Follies and nonsense, whims and inconsistencies *do* divert me, I own, and I laugh at them whenever I can." (*P & P*, 42) Jane is contrasted with Elizabeth in terms of a lack of critical judgment. Elizabeth remarks to her:

10

*"Oh! you are a great deal too apt you know, to like people
in general. You never see a fault in anybody. All the world
are good and agreeable in your eyes. I never heard you speak
ill of a human being in my life."* (P & P, 10)

Jane's naivete engenders a sense of responsibility in Elizabeth. Her affection
for her sister takes the form of defensiveness. Elizabeth employs her own
critical powers in Jane's behalf, since Jane is obviously incapable of exercising
any kind of critical ability in her own right. Elizabeth's almost maternal
solicitude for her less intelligent sister coupled with her own prejudice towards
Darcy leads her, ironically, into the intellectual error of trusting the devious
Wickham and of refusing Darcy's first proposal because he "has been the means
of ruining, perhaps for ever, the happiness of a most beloved sister." (P & P,
143)

Jane's lack of intellectual acuity is both a source of conflict for Elizabeth and
an ironic corrective to Elizabeth's tendency to form hasty judgments. When
Elizabeth condemns Charlotte Lucas's marriage and Bingley's behavior, Jane
remarks: "It is very often our own vanity that deceives us." (P & P, 103)
Vanity, in the form of prejudice, later emerges as the very source of Elizabeth's
self-deception.

While Elizabeth comes to agree with Jane that vanity may indeed deceive,
she never shares Jane's placid acceptance of Charlotte Lucas's marriage to Mr.
Collins. Charlotte is a truly conventional woman in her marital choice. She
illustrates perfectly the ironic meaning of the first sentence of *Pride and Prejudice*: "It is a truth universally acknowledged, that a single man in possession of
a good fortune, must be in want of a wife." In her role as a single woman in
want of a husband, Charlotte causes profound distress to Elizabeth because
her choice of Mr. Collins conflicts violently both with Elizabeth's personal
aspirations and with her moral sensitivity.

The friendship of Charlotte and Elizabeth is marked by a note of intellectual
equality which is absent from Elizabeth's relationship with Jane. Like Elizabeth, Charlotte is witty and ironic and enjoys indulging in playful criticism
of society. When Charlotte expresses the conventional, pragmatic view of
marriage Elizabeth is misled by an assumed unanimity of opinion between
herself and her friend and laughingly dismisses the comment.

"Happiness in marriage is entirely a matter of chance. If the

11

dispostions of the parties are ever so well known to each other, or ever so similar before-hand, it does not advance their felicity in the least. They always continue to grow sufficiently unlike afterwards to have their share of vex- ation; and it is better to know as little as possible of the defects of the person with whom you are to pass your life."

"You make me laugh, Charlotte; but it is not sound. You know it is not sound, and that you would never act in this way yourself." (P & P, 16)

When Charlotte, who is twenty-seven and neither handsome nor rich, accepts Mr. Collins from "the pure and disinterested desire of establishment" (*P & P*, 93) Elizabeth is shocked and disappointed. She is convinced that happiness in such a union is impossible for Charlotte and her chagrin at her friend so colors their relationship that no real confidence ever again exists between the two. When Jane attempts to defend Charlotte's action, Elizabeth adopts a stance of cold, principled superiority:

"You shall not defend her, though it is Charlotte Lucas. You shall not, for the sake of one individual, change the meaning of principle and integrity, nor endeavor to persuade yourself or me, that selfishness is prudence, and insensibility of danger, security for hapiness." (P & P, 103)

This condemnation of Charlotte, while illustrative of Elizabeth's intelligence and aspiration, hardly seems appropriate for a heroine of moral sensitivity. But Elizabeth has been deeply wounded and confused by her friend's willful decision to "grow progressively unaware, to reduce herself to simplicity."[24] Moreover, Charlotte's marriage challenges all that Elizabeth values in life and is in direct opposition to all of her personal aspirations.

Elizabeth aspires to happiness in a marriage founded upon love and mutual esteem. Her own refusal of Mr. Collins, in the face of her mother's blatantly obvious wish that she accept him, was based on her belief that he could not make her happy and her conviction that she was the last woman in the world that could make him so. (*P & P*, 81) Her approval of Jane's union with Bingley is based, from the very first, upon the conviction that theirs would be a marriage of "true affection." (*P & P*, 74).

Elizabeth's mother, who parrots the stereotypes of their wealth and status-conscious society, has made Elizabeth uncomfortably aware of the unconventionality of her personal desire for happiness and love in marriage. Charlotte's defection to the marriage-mart mentality comes as another blow to Elizabeth and reveals both the nature of Elizabeth's aspirations and the moral value she attaches to marriage. But just as the uncritical remark of Jane ironically predicts Elizabeth's own failure of insight so, too, Charlotte's marriage discloses the impractical and illusory side of Elizabeth's intellegence. Elizabeth judges Charlotte according to a set of ideal moral principles and, taken abstractly, they are superior to Charlotte's pragmatism. But Elizabeth fails to consider Charlotte's dilemma in terms of her social world; she never once considers the unhappy alternative facing Charlotte--the plight of the old maid. The lot of the old maid, the "redundant woman" in nineteenth century society, has been described this way:

> *Early marriages were the rule, and an unwed woman of thirty was already an object of pity. She took her place in the family as an unsuccessful human being, and though she might be loved and respected by all the household, a bitter drop of condescension was generally mixed with the affection. She became the aunt, the nurse, the useful member of the family who had no responsibilities of her own, the person whom the others could call upon for help in any emergency.*[25]

The fate of the old maid holds no terrors for Emma Woodhouse, handsome, clever and rich, who boasts that " . . . a single woman, of good fortune, is always respectable . . . "(*E*, 58) Emma, the talented heroine, has in her sister Isabella Knightley a conventional figure who serves to elicit her own unconventional attributes as Jane Bennet does for Elizabeth. Isabella perfectly fulfills the stereotyped expectations of her society:

> *Mrs. John Knightley was a pretty, elegant little woman, of gentle, quiet manners, and a disposition remarkably amiable and affectionate; wrapt up in her family; a devoted wife, a doating mother, and so tenderly attached to her father and sister that, but for these higher ties, a warmer*

love might have seemed impossible. She could never see a
fault in any of them. She was not a woman of strong under-
standing or any quickness. (E, 63)

Like Jane Bennet, Isabella is presented as uncritical, unanalytical and imperceptive in comparison with her talented sister. While Jane functions chiefly to display Elizabeth's intelligence, Isabella serves to elicit Emma's moral sensitivity. The complacent Isabella is all but oblivious to the cross reproaches of her uneven-tempered husband, but Emma is not. Her sensitive nature is always on the alert in her sister's behalf and "She was quick in feeling the little injuries to Isabella, which Isabella never felt herself." (E, 63) Knightley compares the two sisters to Isabella's detriment: "Isabella was too much like Emma--differing only in those striking inferiorities, which always brought the other brilliancy before him." (E, 298) Isabella is a less interesting character in her relationship to Emma than Jane is to Elizabeth, largely because she is so obviously established as a foil for her superior sister. She does not, as Jane Bennet and Celia Brooke do, ever expose her sister's deficiencies through unintentional or ironic comment. Perhaps it is well for Emma that Isabella so uncritically foils her, for in Jane Fairfax Emma encounters a character who, all unwittingly, allows Emma to betray her own worst flaws.

Jane Fairfax is, in reality, anything but a conventional woman character. Her clandestine engagement to Frank Churchill is clearly at odds with the social and sexual mores of her society; she is capable of rash and improper behavior, a genuine commitment to passion, and is torn by conflicting feelings.[26] But Jane is seen by her society, and by Emma herself, in the most conventional terms. The adjective which most frequently describes her is "accomplished." "That sweet, amiable Jane Fairfax!" exclaims Isabella, "only Jane Fairfax one knows to be so very accomplished and superior!" (E, 71) For once, Isabella's vapid observations do not distinguish her; everyone in Highbury society is deceived about the true nature of Jane Fairfax.

Just as Charlotte Lucas's marriage contrasts with and so calls attention to Elizabeth's aspirations, Jane Fairfax's unusual reserve functions to reveal Emma's aspirations to power. Jane demonstrates the nature of Emma's aspirations mainly by frustrating them, for one can hardly manipulate a person whom one cannot even approach. Emma harbors a distinct dislike for Jane, partly because she is jealous of Jane's accomplishments--"Mr. Knightley had once told her [Emma] it was because she saw in her [Jane] the really accom-

14

plished young woman, which she wanted to be thought herself." (*E*, 111) But Emma's main objection to Jane is her coldness and reserve. Undaunted, Emma proceeds to construct an imaginary adulterous love affair for Jane, imagines herself in love with Jane's secret fiance, and flirts outrageously with him. When the true nature of Jane's engagement is revealed, Emma is exposed in all her foolishness.

The comparison with Jane Fairfax does not work entirely to Emma's detriment. While she is humiliated, she also grows in self-knowledge. Moreover, Jane's reserve is a moral flaw which serves to accentuate Emma's candor and frankness. As Mr. Knightley, who functions as a moral norm in the novel, expresses it: "Jane Fairfax is a very charming young woman--but not even Jane Fairfax is perfect . . . She has not the open temper which a man would wish for in a wife." (*E*, 195)

The lack of an "open temper" in a wife is the immediate occasion for one of the most complex dilemmas which Dorothea Brooke encounters. The "wife" in question is Rosamund Vincy Lydgate, an accomplished woman in every sense of the word. In the characters of Jane Fairfax and Rosamund we note the association of accomplishment with unnaturalness. Rosamund, while at Mrs. Lemon's school, had practiced such arts as "getting in and out of a carriage." (*M*, 71) Accompanying her many accomplishments is a great sense of herself as a romantic heroine. The narrator tells us that Rosamund even "acted her own character" (*M*, 87) and, when disappointed in love, she is "a charming stage Ariadne left behind with all her boxes full of costumes and no hope of a coach." (*M*, 221)

An artificial, superficial woman and a disloyal wife who delights in the discovery that even after marriage women might make conquests and enslave men, (*M*, 319) Rosamund seems a natural straw figure to foil the serious and talented Dorothea. If Eliot were a less talented writer or if her vision were less compassionate, she might mercilessly and satirically have exposed the moral deficiencies of Rosamund's coquetry while simultaneously exalting the virtues of Dorothea. But Eliot is not so concerned with the element of contrast in the characters of Dorothea and Rosamund, although it is carefully delineated, as she is with the living web of human relationships, the intricate "stealthy convergence of human lots" (*M*, 70) which ironically links the destinies of an apparently heartless flirt and a woman of sincere, if naive, humanitarian ardor.

15

The crucial encounter between Dorothea and Rosamund in Chapter 81 of *Middlemarch* serves to define the nature of Dorothea's aspiration and her moral sensitivity. Her ardent desire to accomplish some real good in her provincial society is offered some fulfillment through Rosamund. Dorothea is able to ease the tension in Rosamund and Lydgate's marriage and, more importantly, she enables Rosamund to perform the first really unselfish act of her life when the latter confesses the true nature of her flirtatious relationship with Will Ladislaw. Rosamund has also provided Dorothea with a searing test of her moral sensitivity; after a night of pain and jealousy, Dorothea is still capable of facing Rosamund for she has achieved, in her dark night of the soul, the moral insight that "the objects of her rescue were not to be sought out by her fancy: they were chosen for her." (*M*, 577)

While Rosamund functions largely to heighten our appreciation of Dorothea's aspiration and sensitivity, she also serves to draw attention to one of Dorothea's deficiencies--her naivete. The adulterous relationship which Dorothea presumes to exist between Will and Rosamund is her first true personal encounter with evil and the struggle which this initial knowledge of evil causes her exposes the real quixoticism of her character. Celia Brooke performs a role similar to Rosamund's in that she, with her practical and uncomplex vision, often reveals the blindnesses which are inherent in Dorothea's intellectual ardor.

Dorothea remarks that she is "shortsighted" and Celia's comments serve to illustrate the symbolic significance of this literal truth. Like Jane Bennet and unlike Isabella Woodhouse, Celia is a truly engaging foil for her talented sister: she does not exist as a static figure to display Dorothea's superiority, but rather is a dynamic character who calls attention to Dorothea's deficiencies. Celia is a conventional figure, happy and accomplished, capable of amusing herself by playing " 'an air, with variations,' a small kind of tinkling which symbolised the aesthetic part of the young ladies' education." (*M*, 33)

While Celia lacks Dorothea's intellectual curiosity and religious ardor and seems, in this respect, inferior to her, she offers penetrating and truthful comments upon the dilemma of intellectual ardor. She defines, quite accurately, the essential problem of Dorothea's vision: "You always see what nobody else sees; it is impossible to satisfy you; yet you never see what is quite plain. That's your way, Dodo." (*M*, 27) When Dorothea notices only Casaubon's great soul, Celia undercuts her enthusiasm by remarking his two white moles with hairs on them, his irritating dining habits and his manner of blinking

16

before he speaks. Neither Dorothea's nor Celia's vision is correct or complete. As always in Eliot, the truth about every character is complex and no one person in the novel is ever in possession of the entire truth about another's character. Despite the commonness of Celia's observations, however, she performs a valuable function because she provides an alternative vision to Dorothea's; and when she remarks of Dorothea that "She likes giving up." (*M*, 13) we note that even the most common natures are sometimes capable of prophecy.

The dilemma which the conventional woman can pose for the talented heroine has to this point been discussed in terms of the crises which accompany adulthood: love, courtship and marriage. In the characters of Jane Eyre and Maggie Tulliver we encounter two heroines who have coped with this dilemma since childhood. The beautiful, passive Lucy Deane is a source of conflict for her impulsive and tomboyish cousin Maggie, while the pretty, doll-like Reed sisters torture the physically plain and unconventionally self-assertive Jane Eyre.

The contrast between the conventional Lucy and the hoydenish Maggie is established early in *The Mill on the Floss*:

> *Maggie had thrown her bonnet off very carelessly, and, coming in with her hair rough as well as out of curl, rushed at once to Lucy, who was standing by her mother's knee. Certainly the contrast between the cousins was conspicuous . . . It was like the contrast between a rough, dark, overgrown puppy and a white kitten.* (MF, 55)

Maggie is enchanted by Lucy and imagines wistfully that she herself might be the queen in a perennial world of childhood only in Lucy's form. This latent and frustrated envy of Lucy expresses itself in the episode of the hair-cutting and in Maggie's impulsive attempt to dethrone Lucy by pushing her into the mud.

Jane Eyre is also contrasted unfavorably with the conventional prettiness of Georgiana and Eliza Reed. The nursemaid Abbot remarks of Jane, "If she were a nice, pretty child, one might compassionate her forlornness; but one cannot really care for such a little toad as that." (*JE*, 21) Eliza and Georgiana, in contrast, are "dressed out in thin muslin frocks and scarlet sashes, with hair

17

elaborately ringletted." (*JE*, 23) While Jane finds her solace in reading tales of adventure and romance, Georgiana amuses herself by "dressing her hair at the glass, and interweaving her curls with artificial flowers and faded feathers." (*JE*, 25) Even "little toads," however, can have a sense of self-esteem and a need for self-assertion. Not unlike Maggie, Jane expresses her frustration through a physical assault upon John Reed and a verbal condemnation of Mrs. Reed:

> *"You think I have no feelings, and that I can do without one bit of love or kindness; but I cannot live so: and you have no pity . . . People think you are a good woman, but you are bad; hard-hearted.* You *are deceitful."* (JE, *31)*

Jane and Maggie are humiliated in childhood because they depart from the conventional expectations of their elders. Both are frustrated by cousins who fulfill these stereotyped expectations and both display a sense of self-assertion and a capacity for passion in their reactions to frustration. As adults, Maggie and Jane renew their contact with the sources of their childhhod sufferings.

As a young lady, Lucy has more than fulfilled the promises of her childhood. From a doll-like conventional child she has grown to be a neat little lady who embroiders beautifully, flirts gracefully, and dutifully accompanies her fiance Stephen in a musical rendition of "Graceful Consort." Indeed, in her accomplished flirtation with Stephen she has affinities with Rosamund Vincy. Stephen assesses Lucy's character in terms remarkably like Lydgate's description of Rosamund:

> *. . . perhaps he [Stephen] approved his own choice of her [Lucy] because she did not strike him as a remarkable rarity. A man likes his wife to be pretty: well, Lucy was pretty, but not to a maddening extent. A man likes his wife to be accomplished, gentle, affectionate, and not stupid; and Lucy had all these qualifications.* (MF, *323)*

The great difference between Rosamund and Lucy lies in the moral callousness of the former and the naive, open-hearted benevolence of the latter. Despite her outward conformity to the conventions of her world, Lucy possesses the inner moral strength to grow beyond their narrowness, as her relationship with Maggie indicates.

Perhaps it is succinctly symbolic of the great difference between Maggie and Lucy that Lucy wishes Maggie to wear her own large jet broach because "that little butterfly looks silly on you." (*MF*, 325) Indeed, Maggie's lot has been anything but the gay, ornamental one of the butterfly. She has suffered years of privation since her father's bankruptcy, has eagerly adopted the doctrine of renunciation, and has just completed two years' labor in a dreary schoolroom. Her poverty and apparent self-discipline have given her an aspect of sincerity and seriousness which distinguishes her from other women. Stephen Guest is quick to note this and expresses his perception in a way not dissimilar to Lydgate's initial assessment of Dorothea: " 'Too tall,' said Stephen, smiling down upon her [Lucy] , 'and a little too fiery. She is not my type of woman, you know.' " (*MF*, 332) Lydgate judges the a-typical Dorothea:

> *She did not look at things from the proper feminine angle.*
> *The society of such women was about as relaxing as going*
> *from your work to teach the second form, instead of reclin-*
> *ing in a paradise with sweet laughs for bird-notes, and blue*
> *eyes for a heaven.* (M, 70)

Rosamund and Lucy, superficially alike in their conventionality and widely separated by the great gulf of moral sensitivity, do share a common function. Each of them elicits the best moral qualities of the talented heroine and enables her to sacrifice her private wishes to a greater good. Dorothea is roused from her personal grief by a recognition of Rosamund's need; Maggie makes her crucial decision to leave Stephen because of a fidelity to the past--a past which includes Lucy--and an unwillingness to purchase her own happiness at the price of Lucy's misery.

Jane Eyre's reunion with Eliza and Georgiana Reed is most unlike Maggie's adult relationship to Lucy and is less engaging and satisfying. The Reed girls have evolved from selfish, spoiled children to cold, repulsive women. Eliza has become a stern ascetic, and eventually enters a convent. Georgiana is a self-indulgent, blowsy, sentimental monster: ". . . a full-blown, very plump damsel, fair as wax-work; with handsome and regular features, languishing blue eyes, and ringleted yellow hair." (*JE*, 200) In their obvious vulgarity, they cannot but function as sickly foils to Jane's superiority. The Reed sisters are even less satisfactory as foils than Isabella Knightley is to Emma, for one has the disquieting feeling that almost anyone would appear superior when compared to Eliza and Georgiana.

19

What is perhaps most disturbing in the presentation of the Reed sisters is the obvious triumph for Jane which their degeneration represents. When we are told that "Georgiana made an advantageous match with a wealthy worn-out man of fashion" (*JE*, 212) the underlying implication is that Providence has vindicated Jane Eyre by overthrowing her enemies. Eliza and Georgiana are, however, useful figures in their symbolic functions. Each represents an extreme --Eliza is all judgment, Georgiana all feeling and sentiment--which Jane must learn to avoid. They remind us of the talented heroine's need to achieve a delicate poise and of the dangers of the absolute stance.

The fate assigned to Georgiana is not surprising when one considers the suspect view of beauty in *Jane Eyre*. The accomplished Rosamund Oliver possesses perfect beauty, ". . . no charm was wanting, no defect perceptible" (*JE*, 319), but she is exposed as a well-meaning but simple-minded earthly angel. In the implied connection of beauty and accomplishment with giddiness and thoughtlessness or with a lack of moral sensitivity, she is in the pattern of Jane Fairfax, Rosamund Vincy, and Georgiana Reed. It is tempting to place Lucy Deane, at least superficially, within this category, for her simplicity sometimes attains the level of Rosamund Oliver's. But the judgment upon Rosamund is the private one of Jane Eyre's and is, in a sense, an extension of Jane's self-image.

It is to the self-image and self-definition of each of the talented heroines that we must next turn our attention. Some of the "levels of female incompetence" which Eliot described as "various" have been portrayed through an examination of the limitations of the conventional woman and the effects of her stereotyped nature upon the talented heroines. The dilemma of talent is, however, more than an external phenomenon. It can be illustrated to some degree by a comparison of talent with accomplishment, but the roots of the dilemma lie in each heroine's unique concept of the self.

Chapter 2

IMAGES OF THE SELF:
THE POSITIVE IMAGE

When Mr. Knightley, in Jane Austen's *Emma*, begins to suspect a real attachment between Jane Fairfax and Frank Churchill, he sternly qualifies his suspicion by remembering a line from Cowper's poem "The Task": "Myself creating what I saw." (*E*, 234) This line of Cowper's points to one of the major dilemmas of the talented heroine. Each heroine, to some degree, employs her moral sensitivity and intellectual acuity to create an image of her world and of the people who inhabit it. The image the heroine has of her society is to a large extent a product of the image she holds of herself. Hence, Elizabeth Bennet's defensiveness causes her to view her materialistic society as threatening, while Emma's self-confidence permits her to see her world as one which she can easily dominate and manipulate. The young Maggie Tulliver and Jane Eyre, because of their sense of themselves as outcast and alien, tend to perceive their worlds and the adults who dominate them as dangerous and hostile. Dorothea Brooke's negative image of herself as ignorant and unfulfilled is certainly instrumental in causing her to create the illusion of Mr. Casaubon as teacher, inspirer and a potential source of her own self-fulfillment.

In considering the dilemma of the talented heroine, it is tempting to view her as a victim of a repressive society which thwarts her aspirations and prevents her from achieving complete self-fulfillment. This interpretation is especially appealing when one considers the dilemmas of George Eliot's heroines, Maggie Tulliver and Dorothea Brooke. Dorothea, the later-born St. Theresa, can be sympathetically and simplistically viewed as the victim of her unheroic, provincial world. Similarly, it is convenient and comfortable to see in Maggie Tulliver a martyr to the unimaginative, secular Dodson standards. Such over-simplifications as these, however, ignore the complexity of the heroines' dilemma by failing to consider the degree to which self-image, education, personal moral flaws and society itself unite to affect the heroines in their respective searches for self-fulfillment.

George Eliot reminds us of the need to consider how the complex interaction of various forces works to shape her characters' lives. While she admits, for example, that the "sordid" life of the Tullivers and Dodsons does have a stultifying effect upon Tom and Maggie—"I share with you this sense of oppressive narrowness; but it is necessary that we should feel it, if we care to understand how it acted on the lives of Tom and Maggie" (*MF*, 238)—she also reminds us that Maggie's inadequate education has provided fertile soil for the growth of certain moral flaws. Maggie, we are told, was "quite without that knowledge of the irreversible laws within and without her, which, governing the habits, becomes morality, and , developing the feelings of submission and dependence, becomes religion." (*MF*, 252-253)

A possible corrective to the simplistic view of character which Eliot implicitly warns against can be found in a thorough examination of the self-images of the talented heroines. It is useful to return to Cowper's poem and to note the context of the lines which Mr. Knightley applied to himself, "Myself creating what I saw":

> *Me oft has fancy, ludicrous and*
> *wild,*
> *Sooth'd with a waking dream of*
> *houses, tow'rs,*
> *Trees, churches, and strange visages,*
> *express'd*
> *In the red cinders, while with poring*
> *eye*
> *I gaz'd, myself creating what I saw.*[1]

It is interesting to note that the speaker in the poem attributes his imaginative vision to "fancy" and that "fancy" is pejoratively described as "ludicrous and wild." Fancy provides an escape for the speaker but he recognizes his vision to be illusory: the clear implication is that "what I saw," the end product of his creation, lacks correspondence with the mundane realities of the winter evening.

The five talented heroines, like the speaker in "The Task," create what they see, not through the medium of red cinders, but through the lenses of their own self-images. They have an additional affinity with Cowper's persona in that each of them eventually confronts the problem of illusion vs. reality. While Cowper's persona is aware from the first that his creation is illusory, the talented heroine is unaware: her self-image is mainly unconscious. The degree to which illusion has distorted her self-image becomes conscious to her only as she attains, whether suddenly or gradually, the necessary degree of self-knowledge.

Self-image may be considered to be the subconscious or unconscious way in which the heroine views herself, the value which she places upon herself as a person and her estimate of her own worth. The term "image" has been chosen in preference to such words as "self-esteem" or "self-concept" because it gives a clearer sense of the complexity of the heroines' dilemma. Elizabeth, Emma, Jane, Dorothea and Maggie are intellectually acute and they are gifted with an active imaginative sense. Their conduct, speech and meditation reveal that they think of themselves less frequently in terms of simple polarities such as good and bad, worthy and unworthy, than they do in terms of a pervasive, imagistic concept of self.

It is, for example, obvious to us that Emma has consciously "good" feelings about herself: she recognizes that she is a dutiful daughter, a faithful sister and a benevolent benefactor of the poor in her parish. Not immediately perceptible to the reader, however, is the pervasive and unconscious image of herself as a benign manipulator which underlies Emma's positive feelings. Similarly, it is apparent that Elizabeth Bennet exhibits "bad" or negative thoughts about herself when she realizes how she has mistaken Darcy's character. Further examination reveals that the intensity of Elizabeth's self-condemnation derives not simply from a moral judgment but from the realization that she had unconsciously imaged herself as a detached and correct perceiver; her new self-knowledge suddenly makes her painfully aware of this self-image and of its illusory nature.

As Elizabeth's case indicates, the self-image of the heroine is not necessarily static and stable. The talented heroine is dynamic, intelligent, sensitive and imaginative and her self-image alters as she grows in self-knowledge. Jane Eyre, for example, sees herself variously as a rebel, as unconventional and as a moral norm. Dorothea Brooke's self-image progresses from the view of the self as inadequate and needing fulfillment, to the image of the self as consoler and, finally, to the image of the self as a source of fulfillment for others. Maggie Tulliver's self-image alters from one of the self as alien, to the self as ascetic and finally reverts to the dominant image of the self as child.

The self-image of the talented heroine reveals an internal aspect of the dilemma of talent. We have seen how the conventional women characters pose various kinds of external threats to the aspirations and sensibilities of the talented heroine, and how this conventionality often frustrates and complicates the unconventional heroine's search for self-fulfillment. It is vital to the understanding of the full dimension of the dilemma of talent that we turn to the heroines' inner selves. It is true, for example, that the external event of Charlotte Lucas's marriage prompts a revelation of Elizabeth Bennet's unconventionality when she reacts with disgust and disapproval. This observation tells something about the social nature of Elizabeth's dilemma, but it reveals relatively little about the interior struggle of this talented heroine. We wish to know why Elizabeth reacts this way, what the nature and source of her self-image is and how this self-image is related to her demonstrated qualities of intellectual acuity, moral sensitivity and a sense of aspiration.

ELIZABETH BENNET

Elizabeth Bennet and Emma Woodhouse possess self-images which are positive but illusory. Elizabeth's predominant self-image is of herself as the detached, discriminating truth-perceiver in a society where folly predominates. She remarks to Darcy: "Follies and nonsense, whims and inconsistencies *do* divert me, I own, and I laugh at them whenever I can." (*P & P*, 42) The ability to laugh implies a certain detachment of self from society on Elizabeth's part, as well as an assumption of superiority. This sense of superiority stems from Elizabeth's conscious delight in her own intellectual acuity, and it is demonstrated in her repartee with the mild and relatively impercipient Mr. Bingley:

> *"Whatever I do is done in a hurry," replied he [Bingley]: "and therefore if I should resolve to quit Netherfield, I should probably be off in five minutes. At present, however, I consider myself as quite fixed here."*

24

> *"That is exactly what I should have supposed of you,"* said
> Elizabeth.
> *"You begin to comprehend me, do you?"* cried he, turning
> towards her.
> *"Oh! yes--I understand you perfectly."*
> *"I wish I might take this for a compliment; but to be so easily
> seen through I am afraid is pitiful."*
> *"That is as it happens. It does not necessarily follow that a
> deep, intricate character is more or less estimable than such
> a one as yours."*
> . . . *"I did not know before,"* continued Bingley immediate-
> ly, *"that you were a studier of character. It must be an
> amusing study."*
> *"Yes; but intricate characters are the* most *amusing. They
> have at least that advantage."* (P & P, 31)

Elizabeth's dialogue with Bingley reveals several aspects of her self-image. Her
self-confidence enables her to be most unconventionally self-assertive towards
a gentleman whom her society values highly since he possesses a fortune and
must therefore be in want of a wife. Her delight in exercising her wit, almost to
the point of insult, illustrates clearly the influence of her father's philosophy:
"For what do we live, but to make sport for our neighbours, and laugh at
them in our turn?" (P & P, 272) Finally and most importantly, we note
Elizabeth's pleasure at being styled a "studier of character" and her witty
but insensitive display of her powers of discrimination when she clearly implies
that of the two classes of characters–the deep and intricate and the simplistic
--Bingley's belongs to the latter.

Elizabeth's interior image of herself as a detached perceiver stems partly from
a need for some method of self-defense. Her mother and all of her sisters
except Jane, are a constant source of embarrassment to her in their vulgarity,
ignorance and unabashed devotion to meanly materialistic values. When she
attends the ball at Netherfield, Elizabeth immediately detaches herself from
her mother, both physically and mentally. While musing upon the idea that a
marriage between Jane and Bingley would be a felicitous match, Elizabeth
notes that: "Her mother's thoughts . . . were bent the same way, and she
[Elizabeth] determined not to venture near her, lest she might hear too much."
(P & P, 75) Elizabeth's efforts at detachment are, however, not entirely successful. She suffers "agonies" of mortification during her sister Mary's weak

and affected musical rendition and mentally concludes:

> *. . . had her family made an agreement to expose themselves as much as they could during the evening, it would have been impossible for them to play their parts with more spirit, or finer success.* (P & P, 77)

After Darcy has delivered his famous insult, Elizabeth assumes a detached stance as a method of self-defense. Her defensiveness stems not so much from an imperious nature as it does from a sense of vulnerability. She is quite rightly aware that her family's conduct renders her open to insult; her chosen method of defense is her characteristically wry, ironic one:

> *She told the story [of Darcy's insult] . . . with great spirit among her friends; for she had a lively, playful disposition, which delighted in any thing ridiculous.* (P & P, 8)

By telling the story herself, Elizabeth gains a measure of control over the situation because she establishes herself as the perceiver and interpreter of the incident.

The scene of Mr. Collins' proposal clearly illustrates Elizabeth's use of detachment as defense. When his pompous letter is read to the family Elizabeth does not, as do her sisters, engage in speculation about the meaning and implications behind the purple prose. Instead, she judges the intellect of the man who could write in such a way and rhetorically asks her father, "Can he be a sensible man, sir?" (P & P, 48) Her query not only illustrates the premium which she places upon intelligence, but also hints that Elizabeth may be mentally preparing a defense against Mrs. Bennet's perpetual match-making ambitions. The proposal scene itself illustrates Elizabeth's unconventionality, her sense of self-esteem and her aspiration to happiness in a marriage based upon mutual love and respect. The proposal also elicits her characteristic method of defense when her moral sensibility is outraged. Elizageth detaches herself from the situation by reducing Mr. Collins to a kind of "comic monster":[2]

> *The idea of Mr. Collins, with all his solemn composure, being run away with by his feelings, made Elizabeth so near laughing that she could not use the short pause he allowed in any attempt to stop him farther.* (P & P, 80)

Elizabeth's image of herself as a perceiver is related to her intellectual acuity and her moral sensitivity and, while she has illusions about her omniscience, she is often extremely accurate. Elizabeth alone has the perception to realize the dangers to which her sister Lydia's "high animal spirits" may lead. In a decided and self-assured manner, Elizabeth entreats her father to exercise his parental authority by forbidding Lydia's journey to Brighton:

> *"Our importance, our respectability in the world, must be affected by the wild volatility, the assurance and disdain of all restraint which mark Lydia's character . . . If you, my dear father, will not take the trouble of checking her exuberant spirits, and of teaching her that her present pursuits are not to be the business of her life, she will soon be beyond the reach of amendment. Her character will be fixed, and she will, at sixteen, be the most determined flirt that ever made herself and her family ridiculous."* (P & P, 173)

Elizabeth sounds sharp and opinionated but she is entirely correct. Her perception of Lydia's nature is vindicated by subsequent events: Lydia's elopement with Wickham, the hasty marriage and Lydia's shameless flaunting of her married state upon her return to Longbourn. The authoritative tone with which Elizabeth addresses her father is not disrespectful; indeed, her vehemence illustrates another aspect of her perception. She "had never been blind to the impropriety of her father's behavior as a husband" (P & P, 117) and she is painfully aware that the utmost pressure is needed in her effort to exert Mr. Bennet to exercise his paternal responsibilities.

Elizabeth is so often proved correct in her perceptions that it is not difficult to understand why she holds the unconscious image of herself as perceiver. She is most engaging as a character, however, when her judgments are incorrect; her three great mistakes--her assessments of Charlotte's marriage, of Wickham's character, of Darcy's character--occur when she abandons the detached stance and becomes emotionally involved.

Elizabeth's self-image is certainly at the heart of her mistaken assessment of Charlotte's marriage. Her categorical condemnation of Charlotte is based on the assumption that she, Elizabeth, has powers of discernment and perception which are superior to Charlotte's. The possibility that Charlotte's pragmatic principles may be as judicious in terms of Charlotte's aspirations as Elizabeth's ideal principles are for her simply does not occur to Elizabeth. The notion of the relativity of personal values is unacceptable to Elizabeth in her doctrinaire conviction that it is impossible for Charlotte to be even "tolerably happy" in the lot she has chosen.

When Elizabeth first visits Charlotte after the latter's marriage, she attains a dim realization of the illusory nature of her own self-image. To be sure, Charlotte is not ideally happy. Mr. Collins' remarks often embarrass her, she has chosen an unappealing room for entertaining precisely because her husband will be less likely to frequent it, and her active encouragement of Mr. Collins' gardening betrays more than a wifely concern for his health. Nevertheless, Charlotte is comfortable and she is proud of her home. In short, she is exactly what Elizabeth had so authoritatively decreed impossible: Charlotte has fulfilled her own aspirations, she has a pleasant home and is indeed "tolerably happy." That night, Elizabeth re-evaluates and modifies her earlier judgment:

> . . . Elizabeth in the solitude of her chamber had to meditate upon Charlotte's degree of contentment, to understand her address in guiding, and composure in bearing with her husband, and to acknowledge that it was all done very well. (P & P, 119)

This reassessment of Charlotte's condition does not indicate any substantial growth in self-knowledge on Elizabeth's part. She seems to regard the contented state of life at the parsonage as an inexplicably fortuitous result of Charlotte's mistaken choice. Elizabeth neither questions her own previous assumptions about Charlotte, nor does she doubt her wisdom in judging her friend in terms of her own personal principles and aspirations. A much more personal and painful mistake is required to awaken Elizabeth to her illusory self-image; it is provided in her erroneous assessments of Wickham and Darcy.

The appeal which Wickham initially holds for Elizabeth is not difficult to understand. Although Elizabeth often displays a maturity beyond her years, it is important to remember that she is a high-spirited young woman, still smarting from Darcy's gratuitous insult and susceptible to the flattering attentions of an attractive well-spoken young officer. Wickham's real appeal, however, is on a far deeper level than that of superficial attractiveness. He wins Elizabeth's interest by stimulating her intelluctual curiosity; he attains her friendship by appealing to a strong component of her morally sensitive nature--her sense of justice.

28

It has been noted, in the instance of Elizabeth's narrating the story of Darcy's insult, how she likes to control situations. When she first meets Wickham, Elizabeth is undoubtedly confused about the character of Mr. Darcy. His insulting remark at the Netherfield assembly has been followed by strangely civil and attentive behavior to her at the Bingley home. Elizabeth values complete knowledge as the surest means of control and Wickham appears to be the source who, in explaining Darcy's character, will provide Elizabeth with a needed sense of control and strengthen her unconscious image of herself as perceiver. Because of her strong prejudice towards Darcy, Elizabeth is predisposed to accept uncritically Wickham's slanderous account of Darcy's character. Moreover, her superficial admiration for Wickham predisposes her to sympathize readily with his alleged suffering from Darcy's manifold "injustices."

Wickham's story satisfies Elizabeth's need for control and knowledge. When she relates the substance of his narrative to Jane, Elizabeth's trust in the rectitude of her own judgment is revealed. Jane characteristically responds to this tale of apparent evil with confusion and indecision: "It is difficult indeed --it is distressing. --One does not know what to think." Elizabeth replies with sharp certainty, "I beg your pardon;--one knows exactly what to think" and she looks to the Netherfield ball as an opportunity for confirming her new "knowledge" of Darcy. (P & P, 65)

The ironic truth, of course, is that Elizabeth does not know "what to think," much less "exactly." Her vision of Darcy has been distorted ever since his refusal to dance with her at the Netherfield assembly. In her vulnerability and defensiveness, Elizabeth never pauses to reflect upon Darcy's possible motivation. Howard Babb has noted how Darcy's tone "reveals the instinctive irritation of a shy person at an aggressive invasion of his privacy" rather than betraying "an absolute contempt engendered by pride."[3] It is also possible that Darcy, like Elizabeth, is on the defensive. He is, after all, "a single man in possession of a good fortune" (P & P, 1) and he must be acutely aware that society considers him to be in want of a wife. Elizabeth is an unmarried girl of no fortune, her mother takes no pains to conceal her anxiety to see her daughters married, and Mr. Bingley's words to Darcy about Elizabeth could be interpreted as the clumsiest kind of match-making:

> "But there is one of her [Jane Bennet's] sisters [i.e.,
> Elizabeth] sitting down just behind you, who is
> very pretty, and I dare say, very agreeable. Do let

me ask my partner to introduce you." (P & P, 7)

It is not unlikely that Darcy, like Elizabeth herself, reacts defensively because he resents even the slightest implication that he is but another available commodity in the marriage market of a provincial, materialistic society.

Despite Darcy's attentive treatment when Jane was ill at the Bingley's, Elizabeth retains her initial impression of Darcy as haughty, arrogant and thoroughly disagreeable. She clings to this estimation of him for a number of reasons: she is strengthened in her prejudice by Wickham's story, she believes Darcy to have maliciously separated Bingley and Jane, and she enjoys capitalizing upon her prejudice and exploiting it to display her wit and intelligence. After Darcy's true character is known to her Elizabeth confesses to Jane:

> *"And yet I meant to be so uncommonly clever in taking so decided a dislike to him, without any reason. It is such a spur to one's genius, such an opening for wit to have a dislike of that kind. One may be continually abusive without saying any thing just; but one cannot always be laughing at a man without now and then stumbling on something witty."*
> (P & P, 168)

Darcy's letter of explanation and self-vindication following Elizabeth's indignant rejection of his first proposal is the immediate cause of a great growth in self-knowledge on Elizabeth's part. She learns at once of Wickham's true character, that Charlotte was correct in criticizing Jane's excessive diffidence, and of the sincerity of Darcy's affection. Most importantly, Elizabeth becomes aware of her unconscious image of herself as the omniscient perceiver and of the illusory nature of this self-image. The passage which relates Elizabeth's moment of insight has often been quoted, but it is useful to examine its rhetoric in terms of the many references to perception, sight and knowledge:

> *"How despicably have I acted!"* she cried.--*"I, who have prided myself on my discernment!--I, who have valued myself on my abilities! who have often disdained the generous candour of my sister, and gratified my vanity, in useless or blameable distrust.--How humiliating is this discovery! --Yet, how just a humiliation!--Had I been in love, I could not have been more wretchedly blind. But vanity, not love,*

has been my folly.--Pleased with the preference of one, and offended by the neglect of the other, on the very beginning of our acquaintance, I have courted prepossession *and* ignorance, *and driven* reason *away, where either were concerned. Till this moment, I never* knew *myself." (P & P, 156. Emphasis added)*

The irony of this passage, providing a relief from the heavy tone of self-condemnation, is that Elizabeth still lacks complete self-knowledge. She *is* in love with Darcy and she remains blind to that reality for some time. But, most importantly, Elizabeth now knows what she is *not*. She is not omniscient, infallible or totally detached. Rather, she begins to perceive herself as imperfect, fallible, and intimately involved, for good or ill, with her family's fate. The old skin has been shed, her illusory self-image rejected, and the way to self-fulfillment lies open.

EMMA WOODHOUSE

Elizabeth Bennet was considered by Jane Austen to be "as delightful a creature as ever appeared in print"[4] while Emma Woodhouse was described by her creator as "a heroine whom no one but myself will much like."[5] Indeed it is difficult to imagine two heroines whose situations are more apparently unlike. Elizabeth, lacking fortune and the prestige of good family connections, has only her wit and native intelligence with which to combat the cruelties of her class-conscious society. Emma Woodhouse is the pampered darling of her father, the pride of her doting governess and the acknowledged queen of Highbury society. Despite the great disparities in their respective situations however, Emma and Elizabeth have a good deal in common. Like Elizabeth, Emma has an essentially positive but illusory self-image. Her image of herself as a benign manipulator causes Emma to make serious mistakes in judgment about other people. Like Elizabeth, Emma painfully attains self-knowledge and eventually realizes the illusory nature of her own self-image.

The positive nature of Emma's self-image is clearly established at the very beginning of the novel. Possessing all of the attractive external qualities valued by her society--she is "handsome, clever, and rich" (*E*, 1)--Emma also has an inner serenity and self-contentment from having "lived nearly twenty-one years in the world with very little to distress or vex her." Emma's great faith in her own good judgment has never been reproved or challenged, and she has the habit of "doing just what she liked." Obviously, Emma is a kind of moral infant: her powers of self-control, responsibility and moral sensitivity have neither been developed nor strengthened because she has never encountered any of the repressive and self-correcting crises which normally accompany adulthood. It is no wonder that Emma has a "happy disposition"; she enjoys the infant's narcissistic egoism which George Eliot describes as a state of "moral stupidity, taking the world as an udder to feed our supreme selves." (*M*, 156) Jane Austen succinctly delineates the self-image of Emma in this state of moral infancy:

> *The real evils indeed of Emma's situation were the power of having rather too much her own way, and a disposition to think a little too well of herself; these were the disadvantages which threatened alloy to her many enjoyments. The danger, however, was at present so unperceived, that they did not by any means rank as misfortunes with her.* (E, 1. *Emphasis added*)

It does indeed seem that Emma is the kind of heroine whom it will be difficult to like. But several factors unite to modify the reader's initially negative reaction to this young egoist. Jane Austen makes it apparent that Emma cannot be held solely responsible for her egoism. Her positive and unqualified self-approval is largely an internalization of the opinions which her father and Miss Weston hold of her. Mr. Woodhouse has been a most affectionate, ineffectual, and indulgent father; Miss Weston has implicitly approved of Emma by allowing her to do just what she liked. In short, Emma's "moral stupidity" has been reinforced by the very people who have had the duty of educating her into adulthood.

Another factor which qualifies any tendency wholly to condemn Emma is the fact that her positive self-image is unconscious, "unperceived." Emma is not a committed egoist, nor is she consciously aware that the superiority she feels is in any way illusory or morally suspect. Finally, Jane Austen precludes any immediate condemnation of Emma by implying that her situation is a potentially interesting one: real evils are an inherent part of her self-satisfaction and unperceived danger threatens alloy to her many enjoyments. Emma's situation engages the reader because its many possibilities arouse our curiosity. Like Mr. Knightley, we feel that "There is an anxiety, a curiosity in what one feels for Emma. I wonder what will become of her!" (*E*, 26)

What "becomes" of Emma is that she grows to adulthood and attains a sense of moral sensitivity and responsibility through the self-knowledge which a series of mistaken judgments forces upon her. Her incorrect and impercipient assessments of Harriet Smith and Mr. Elton, Jane Fairfax and Frank Churchill, and Mr. Knightley reveal different facets of her predominant image of herself as a benign manipulator; her many mistaken evaluations serve also to illustrate the variety of problems which aspirtation and intellectuality can pose for the talented heroine.

"Emma never thinks of herself, if she can do good to others;" Mr. Woodhouse declares (E, 7) and indeed his statement expresses Emma's own evaluation of her relationship with Harriet Smith. A mild, bland girl, the "natural daughter of somebody," Harriet is the perfect clay which Emma's artistic imagination can mold into a pleasing creation.

> She [Emma] would notice her [Harriet]; she would improve her; she would detach her from her bad acquaintance, and introduce her into good society; she would form her opinions and her manners. It would be an interesting, and certainly a very kind undertaking; highly becoming her own situation in life, her leisure, and powers. (E, 14)

The illusory nature of Emma's image of herself as Harriet's benign and selfless patron is clearly revealed. Emma stands to profit from her patronage of Harriet to a far greater degree than does Harriet. Forming Harriet's character will be "interesting"; it will relieve some of the boredom of Emma's existence and will help to fill the void created by Miss Weston's departure from the household. Her planned exertions on Harriet's behalf will also be "kind" and "becoming"; they will reflect favorably upon Emma and increase her already considerable sense of self-esteem. Finally, Harriet will provide Emma with an opportunity to fulfill her aspiration to power; the shy, unassuming Harriet will be transformed into a socially acceptable young lady through the selfless attentions of the clever Miss Woodhouse.

Emma proceeds to exercise her benign influence upon Harriet by persuading her to reject the proposal of the eminently suitable Robert Martin on the grounds that he is Harriet's social inferior. Not content with this "achievement," Emma's fertile imagination soon creates a wholly illusory romance between Harriet and Mr. Elton, the vicar of Highbury. Enjoying the heady satisfaction of "a mind delighted with its own ideas" (E, 14) Emma does indeed create what she sees in the instance of the Elton-Harriet "romance." Her chief error is that, in her desire to dominate by providing what she deems a useful service for the two, Emma totally neglects to consider Harriet and Mr. Elton as persons. She views Harriet as "useful," as a valuable "addition to her privileges," and as a convenient model for the display of her own artistic talents.

The portrait which Emma draws of Harriet is a concrete image of her impersonal way of perceiving both Harriet and Mr. Elton. While Harriet is sitting for her portrait, Emma is in perfect control. Harriet is the passive object upon which Emma exercises both her artistry and her imagination. The portrait which emerges is not a likeness of Harriet but a reflection of Emma's own ambitions for Harriet. This is unconsciously revealed in Emma's own meditation upon the picture:

> *The sitting was altogether very satisfactory; she [Emma] was quite enough pleased with the first day's sketch to wish to go on. There was no want of likeness, she had been fortunate in the attitude, and as she meant to throw in a little* improvement *to the figure, to* give a little more height, *and considerably more* elegance, *she had great confidence of its being in every way a pretty drawing at last, and of its filling its destined place with credit to them both--a standing memorial of the beauty of one [Harriet], the skill of the other [Emma], and the* friendship *of both; with as many agreeable associations as Mr. Elton's very promising attachment was likely to add.* (E, 30. Emphasis added)

Emma's intent to improve the picture of Harriet corresponds to her aspiration to educate the girl in real life; her desire to add height to the artistic image of Harriet illustrates her desire to elevate Harriet through a marriage between Harriet and Mr. Elton. Her interpretation of the portrait as a tribute to her friendship with Harriet reveals how unconscious her image of Harriet-as-object is. Emma fancies what is in reality a subject-object relationship to be the reciprocal relationship which constitutes true friendship. The sensible Mr. Knightley is quick to perceive the lack of correspondence between the drawing and the real girl. He says more than he knows when he criticizes: "You have made her too tall, Emma." (E, 31) Mr. Elton's pompously gallant reply to Knightley's observation is extremely revelatory for the reader and it should be significant to an intelligent girl like Emma:

"Oh, no! Certainly not too tall; not in the least too tall. Consider, she is sitting down--which naturally presents a different--which in short gives exactly the idea--and the proportions must be preserved, you know. Proportions, fore-shortening.--Oh, no! it gives one exactly the idea of such a height as Miss Smith's. Exactly so indeed!" (E, 31)

This wordy, repetitive and essentially meaningless observation of Mr. Elton's makes absolutely no sense in terms of Harriet's portrait. But Mr. Elton is defending neither the artistry of the drawing nor the beauty of Harriet. Indeed, he views Harriet rather coolly and impersonally. He never once speaks of the real girl, as Knightley does, but talks of her as an artistic object--"such a height as Miss Smith's." Miss Smith is truly incidental to Mr. Elton; he speaks so warmly in defense of Emma herself and his obvious wish is further to ingratiate himself with Emma.

Emma remains oblivious to this truth because, from the first, she has seen Mr. Elton only as an object. To be sure, she thinks she is doing him a great service in uniting him with Harriet. Emma has created a static, objective image of Mr. Elton as Harriet's lover and during the portrait sitting she perceives only that which reinforces her preconceived idea. Emma attributes Elton's positioning himself behind her while she is drawing to a desire to "gaze and gaze again without offence" (E, 30) at Harriet; when the next day's sitting is planned, Emma approvingly notes that Elton begs to return "just as he ought." (E, 30)

Emma pays a mortifying price for her unconscious assessment of Harriet and Elton as the objects of her benign manipulation. Mr. Elton is no mere object; he has aspirations of his own, and these include winning the hand of the wealthy and superior Emma Woodhouse. Emma's insensitive depersonalization of Harriet rebounds upon her with a vengeance for Mr. Elton has adopted Emma's viewpoint of Harriet. He too has seen Harriet as a mere object, has "never cared whether she were dead or alive" (E, 89) except as Emma's "friend." Fortified by Mr. Weston's good wine, he confidently proposes to Emma and unabashedly declares himself her ardent lover.

The proposal scene highlights one of the strongest facets of Emma's self-image: her unconscious assumption of her own superiority. Her indignation at Elton's audacity stems from his assumption that he should "suppose himself her equal in connection or mind." (E, 92) In her outrage, Emma remains blind to the fact that she has been guilty of a comparable error. In planning a

35

match between Elton and Harriet, she has implicitly assumed a social equality between the two. Mr. Elton is not the leader of Highbury society, he is merely the vicar of the provincial parish, but in terms of Highbury social standards he is certainly socially superior to an illegitimate girl lacking both fortune and favorable connections. In her eager desire to exercise her imaginative powers, Emma has lost sight of a very basic assumption of her society: "Every body has their level." (*E*, 90)

Emma's imagination and aspiration have led her into a mortifying error. Her acute intelligence makes her capable of interpreting her mistake in such a way that she advances in self-knowledge and moral sensitivity. As she meditates upon this "wretched business" she considers Harriet, for the first time, as a real person whom she has deceived and who must suffer as a result of this deception:

> *Such a blow for Harriet!--That was the worst of all. Every part of it brought pain and humiliation, of some sort or other; but, compared with the evil to Harriet, all was light; and she would gladly have submitted to feel yet more mistaken--more in error--more disgraced by mis-judgment, than she actually was, could the effects of her blunders have been confined to herself.* (E, 91)

Emma's new moral sensitivity is accompanied by a partial attainment of self-knowledge. She does not become conscious of her predominant image of herself as a benign manipulator. Unaware that she has manipulated two persons as if they were mere objects, she perceives only, that, in this case, she has not acted benignly:

> *It was foolish, it was wrong, to take* so *active a part in bringing any two people together. It was adventuring* too far, *assuming* too much, *making light of what ought to be serious, a trick of what ought to be simple.* (E, 93. Emphasis added)

Emma does not condemn the kind of action which she has taken, but only the degree of fervor with which she has advanced the match. Indeed, she attempts to console herself by remembering how she had prevented Harriet's marriage to Robert Martin:

36

*"There I was quite right. That was well done of me; but there
I should have stopped, and left the rest to time and chance."*
(E, 93)

Emma does, however, resolve "to do such things no more" (*E*, 93) and her
moments of meditative self-criticism resemble the scene in which Elizabeth
Bennet attains self-knowledge and realizes "Till this moment, I never knew
myself." (*P & P*, 156) After this moment of insight, Elizabeth rejects her
illusory self-image and she faces the remaining dilemmas which society, her
aspirations and interpersonal relationships pose for the talented heroine un-
hindered by an unrealistic sense of self. Emma's lot is not so pleasant. Her self-
image is a more complex one than Elizabeth's, because it contains an inherent
contradiction: the illusion that the manipulation of other persons can be
benign. Emma acquires self-knowledge more slowly and painfully than does
Elizabeth. Emma's self-image, which is shown in her desire to dominate and
control, to impose her fictions upon life, is more complicated and perverse
than Elizabeth's pride of judgment.[6] Emma's relationship with Harriet and Mr.
Elton illustrates her image of herself as benign and the illusions which can
result when an active imagination is coupled with such an illusory self-image.
The Harriet-Elton affair also provides the occasion for a growth in moral
sensitivity on Emma's part. Her relationships with Frank Churchill and Jane
Fairfax highlight the manipulative aspect of her self-image and show how an
illusory self-image can distort the intellectual acuity of the talented heroine.

Emma's dislike for Jane Fairfax has previously been mentioned in terms of
the frustration which Jane's reserve poses to Emma's aspirations to power.
Jane also presents a challenge to Emma's self-image and to her intellectual
acuity. The manipulative personality characteristically strives to control persons and situations. Complete and effective control can only be attained
through the superiority which full knowledge bestows. Emma's intellectual
perceptivity causes her to notice Jane's reserve and uneasiness in social situations and to question Jane's strange preference of a visit to Highbury over a
trip to Ireland. Since Jane herself provides no satisfaction to Emma's curiosity, Emma creates a fiction about Jane which shows the meanest aspect of her
manipulative personality. Emma cleverly develops the idea of a love affair
between Jane and the husband of Jane's friend. She assumes that Jane is
pining after Mr. Dixon and that Jane has refused the visit to Ireland in order
to remove herself from temptation. This cleverly slanderous mental manipulation of Jane so pleases Emma that she exploits it to impress Frank Churchill,
Jane's secret fiance. Emma fancies Frank to be in love with herself and enjoys

engaging in a flirtatious word game in which she and Frank share a private joke concerning Jane's "love" for Mr. Dixon. This situation shows Emma enjoying the height of her illusory manipulative powers. She believes that she is manipulating Jane's feelings when the word *Dixon* is placed before Jane. Emma further imagines that she is manipulating Frank by forcing him to admire her cleverness, thus increasing his supposed affection, while Emma enjoys the secret knowledge that she is planning a match between Frank and Harriet Smith.

Emma attains self-knowledge only when she learns that others have outmanipulated her. Frank Churchill has calculatingly exploited Emma as a blind for his real attachment to Jane; the simple Harriet has unwittingly pained Emma by convincing her that Mr. Knightley is in love with her [Harriet]. When Emma believes that Harriet has won Mr. Knightley's love, her extreme agitation leads to self-knowledge: Emma realizes that she herself has unconsciously been in love with Mr. Knightley. For the first time, Emma experiences strong personal suffering; her meditations during her sorrow conclude with a true insight into self:

> With insufferable vanity had she believed herself in the secret of everybody's feelings; with unpardonable arrogance proposed to arrange everybody's destiny. She was proved to have been universally mistaken; and she had not quite done nothing--for she had done mischief. She had brought evil on Harriet, on herself, and she too much feared, on Mr. Knightley. (E, 284)

At last Emma realizes that she has been a manipulator, that her manipulation has been not benign but arrogant, and that her illusory self-image has caused, not only mischief, but real evil. Chastened and penitent, she is now the morally sensitive heroine who is capable of a fully human integration into her society and deserving of the love of an equally sensitive man.

JANE EYRE

The characters of Emma and Elizabeth Bennet illustrate that a positive self-image is not necessarily a healthy one because positive feelings may be founded upon illusory assumptions. Charlotte Bronte's Jane Eyre shares this positive sense of self with Elizabeth and Emma. Unlike the Austen heroines, however, Jane's self-image is not an illusory one; rather it consistently corresponds to the reality of her situation as the reader perceives it. One source of this close correspondence between self-image and reality can be found in the very structure of the novel. *Jane Eyre* is an autobiography, albeit a selective one, and it is important to realize that Charlotte Bronte envisioned the novel as such. The title page of the 1847 edition of the novel includes the subtitle: *Jane Eyre: An Autobiography.* As G. Armour Craig has pointed out, the world of the autobiography is essentially a private and personal one.[7] The narrator and the heroine share the same vision; hence the kind of irony which arises from Elizabeth's and Emma's incomplete visions is not possible. This is not to say, however, that there is no way in which the reader can distance herself from Jane in order to view her critically. The narrator of the novel, Jane Eyre Rochester, is at least ten years removed in time from the events which she relates and as she reflects upon her past, she herself offers criticisms of her former self.

The lack of illusion in Jane's self-image can also be explained by reference to her self-definition. While Elizabeth and Emma tend to define themselves in terms of fluctuating social relationships and situations, Jane consistently defines herself as a child of God and her standard is the immutable one of Divine Providence. Self-definition, the conscious role or stance which the heroine adopts vis a vis her society, will be explored more thoroughly in another chapter. But it is useful to note at this point that Jane Eyre's world is a providential one where divine justice is clearly manifested to those who see with the eyes of faith.

Because *Jane Eyre* is an autobiography and because the heroine's world is essentially providential, the way in which Jane's self-image consistently corresponds to reality is rendered believable. Once the reader accepts Bronte's "given"—the providential world of the novel—it is easier to comprehend Jane's lack of illusion than it is to understand how she maintains her positive self-image. The source of Jane's positive image of herself is paradoxically a negation: she rejects and refuses to internalize the condemnatory, cruel and sometimes vicious assaults which others make upon her character. The young Maggie Tulliver begins life with a negative self-image precisely because she accepts her family's judgment of herself as "a small mistake of nature." (*MF*, 13) Similarly, it has been noted how, from her childhood through age twenty-one, Emma has internalized the excessively favorable judgments of Mr. Woodhouse and Miss Weston. The young Jane Eyre, however, demonstrates a capacity for self-assertion and a sense of self-esteem which enable her to reject the negative opinions of others. Her initial self-image is of herself as a rebel against the unjust tyrannies of the Reed family. Jane's impulsive attack upon her cousin John is punished by imprisonment in the ghostly red room. Alone and humiliated, Jane entertains the possibility that the adult world might be correct in its judgment: "All said I was wicked, and perhaps I might be so." (*JE*, 13) In a situation which would easily have reduced most other sensitive children to tears of fear and self-reproach, the very most that Jane will grant is that "perhaps" the adult opinion of her may be correct.

It is appropriate that the novel begins with the scene of Jane's first rebellion-- "I resisted all the way: a new thing for me" (*JE*, 9) –because Jane's story is essentially one of resistance to those who attempt to debase her, depersonalize her, or thwart her aspirations to self-fulfillment. Jane's first childhood act of rebellion and self-assertion is followed by a series of like incidents and each punishment prompts a bolder external response from Jane and a greater internal sense of outrage at injustice. When Jane asserts her innate superiority to her cousins by declaring to Mrs. Reed, "They are not fit to associate with me" (*JE*, 22) she is subjected to a physical assault by Mrs. Reed and to a verbal tongue lashing from her nursemaid Bessie:

> *Bessie supplied the hiatus by a homily of an hour's length, in which she proved beyond a doubt that I was the most wicked and abandoned child ever reared under a roof. I* half *believed her; for I felt indeed only bad feelings surging in my breast.* (JE, 23. Emphasis added)

It is significant that, despite the fact that Jane trusts Bessie above any other member of the household, she is nevertheless unwilling to internalize completely the image of herself as a wicked child which Bessie tries to impose.

Jane's final act of rebellion at the Reed home is the speech in which she accuses Mrs. Reed of deceit and characterizes her as "bad" and "hard-hearted." The most important aspect of this speech is its clear revelation of Jane's image of herself as a rebel whose goal is liberty:

> *Ere I had finished this reply my soul began to expand, to exult, with the strangest sense of freedom, of triumph, I*

*ever felt. It seemed as if an invisible bond had burst, and that
I had struggled out into unhoped-for liberty.* (JE, 31)

At the Lowood school Jane retains her hatred of injustice and her rebellious
self-image. She tells Helen Burns:

> *"And if I were in your [Helen's] place I should dislike her; I
> should resist her; if she struck me with that rod, I should get
> it from her hand; I should break it under her nose."* (JE, 48)

Jane's conception of justice is a reflection of her treatment at the Reed home.
The only standards she has been exposed to are the Old Testament laws of
vengeance. Helen introduces Jane, by precept and example, to the New Testament ideal of love and to the doctrine of renunciation:

> *"It is far better to endure patiently a smart which nobody
> feels but yourself, than to commit a hasty action whose evil
> consequences will extend to all connected with you; and,
> besides, the Bible bids us return good for evil."* (JE, 48)

Helen's doctrine of love has a lasting effect upon Jane. Jane's rebelliousness is
tempered by the friendship of Helen and Miss Temple and the self-fulfillment
she eventually finds at the school. With the departure of Miss Temple, however,
Jane again becomes the imprisoned rebel: "I tired of the routine of eight years
in one afternoon. I desired liberty; for liberty I gasped; for liberty I uttered a
prayer." (JE, 74)

Jane does not attain the perfect liberty for which she yearns, but she does
receive her second choice--a "new servitude"--in her position as governess at
Thornfield. Her former image of herself as rebel, largely a product of her moral
sensitivity to injustice, is replaced by a more diffuse sense of herself as unconventional. This new self-image is illustrated most clearly in her relationship with
Mr. Rochester. Rochester is the antithesis of the conventionally well-mannered
gallant hero, and his brusque Byronic moods elicit Jane's own unconventionality. When he asks Jane, "Do you think me handsome? " she replies with a
most unladylike honesty, "No sir." Jane reflects upon her answer:

> *I should, if I had deliberated, have replied to his question
> by something conventionally vague and polite; but the
> answer slipped from my tongue before I was aware.* (JE, 115)

Jane's candor and self-confidence are even more remarkable when one recalls that she not only violates the unwritten etiquette which dictates that flattery should prevail over frankness in male-female relationships, but also that she abandons the traditionally submissive stance of the servant towards her master.

Rochester's conversations with Jane are singularly revelatory of her self-image. He recognizes that Jane is different, particularly in the quality of her mind: "It is a peculiar mind; it is a unique one." (*JE*, 126) Jane listens quietly and with composure to Rochester's sordid tale of his affair with Celine Varens. The stereotyped response for the heroine in this situation would be a display of moral outrage and extreme shock. One has only to recall Mrs. Elton's self-conscious display of her "delicacy" when Jane Fairfax bluntly refers to governesses' placement bureaus as "Offices for the sale--not quite of human flesh--but of human intellect." (*E*, 204) Jane Eyre, however, is quite without stereotyped reactions and is too intelligent to adopt them. Her self-esteem is demonstrated when she interprets Rochester's confidence quite simply as a tribute to her own discretion.

Jane's clearest statement of her positive self-image occurs after Rochester has tortured her with the prospect of his marriage to Blanche Ingram. Her reply reveals her unconventional disregard for social rank and status and her intellectual conviction of her equality, before God, to a man whom society regards as her superior:

> "*Do you think, because I am poor, obscure, plain, and little,*
> *I am soulless and heartless? You think wrong!--I have as much*
> *soul as you,--and full as much heart! . . . I am not talking to*
> *you now through the medium of custom, conventionalities,*
> *nor even of mortal flesh--it is my spirit that addresses your*
> *spirit; just as if both had passed through the grave, and we*
> *stood at God's feet, equal,--as we are!*" (JE, 222)

Jane's only serious struggle with a negative sense of self occurs during the house-party when she first sees Blanche Ingram. Jealousy of Blanche makes Jane aware that she has been nursing a secret love for Rochester. Having caught herself in what she deems to be a hopeless, romantic illusion, Jane derides herself as a mere "dependent and a novice" and a "Poor stupid dupe." She attempts to crush her aspirations to Rochester's love by an unfavorable comparison of herself with Blanche. As it does in *Emma*, art becomes a way of illustrating the heroine's self-image. Jane draws a self-portrait in crayon and paints an ivory miniature of the beautiful Blanche. She plans to compare them whenever she is tempted to forget her "place":

> "Whenever, in future, you should chance to fancy Mr. Rochester thinks well of you, take out these two pictures and compare them: say, 'Mr. Rochester might probably win that noble lady's love, if he chose to strive for it; is it likely he would waste a serious thought on this indigent and insignificant plebian?' " (JE, 141)

This attempt at self-discipline, is, however, ineffectual. Jane has eradicated neither her aspirations nor her positive self-image; she has merely repressed them both. Her moral sensitivity and her intellectual honesty ultimately triumph. Jane judges the artificial Miss Ingram to be morally inferior to herself:

> Miss Ingram was a mark beneath jealousy: she was too inferior to excite the feeling . . . She was very showy, but she was not genuine: she had a fine person, many brilliant attainments; but her mind was poor, her heart barren by nature; nothing bloomed spontaneously on that soil; no unforced natural fruit delighted by its freshness . . . She advocated a high tone of sentiment; but she did not know the sensations of sympathy and pity; tenderness and truth were not in her. (JE, 163)

Jane's critical judgment of Blanche reveals the high premium which Jane places upon naturalness, spontaneity and fidelity to one's true self. Jane faces two crises which test her own ability to be true to her real nature: when Rochester offers her love outside of marriage and when St. John Rivers proposes marriage without love. Each of these dilemmas illustrates the final phase of Jane's evolving self-image: her image of herself as a moral norm.

In refusing Rochester, Jane has only principle and intellectual conviction to guide her. Living abroad with Rochester would result in no social scandal nor, as he reminds her, has she relatives or friends who would be injured. The solution to Jane's dilemma can only be found by looking within herself and taking her own nature as her moral guide. When Rochester asks, "Who in the world cares for *you*? or who will be injured by what you do? " Jane's answer portrays her self-image:

"I care for myself. The more solitary, the more friendless, the more unsustained I am, the more I will respect myself. I will keep the law given by God; sanctioned by man." (JE, 279)

St. John Rivers poses a dilemma for Jane, not because she loves him, but because he appeals to her senses of aspiration and of duty. As a clergyman, St. John should be able to offer some real guidance to Jane. But, in his narrow zealotry, he can only provide his own ambitions under the guise of God's will. Once again, Jane has no norm but the sense of her own integrity and the self-esteem which tells her that marriage without love would be a violation of herself:

> *"I scorn your idea of love,"* I could not help saying, as I rose up and stood before him, leaning my back against the rock. *"I scorn the counterfeit sentiment you offer: yes, St. John, and I scorn you when you offer it."* (JE, 359)

The image of herself as a moral norm is not an indication of conceited moral superiority on Jane's part. Rather it is, like Elizabeth Bennet's detached stance, a way of defending her integrity when it is threatened. When Jane and Rochester are reunited at Ferndean there is no longer any need for defensiveness for theirs is a union based upon equality and mutual love and respect.

Jane's final happiness in her marriage parallels the fulfillment which is predicted for Emma and Elizabeth at the end of their novels. Jane's evolving self-image is demonstrably instrumental in effecting her final happiness; Elizabeth's and Emma's full integration into their respective societies is made possible when they shed their illusory self-images. The five talented heroines share many traits: imagination, intellectuality, aspiration and sensitivity. They also exhibit a wide range of variation in their responses to the problem of self-image. The characters of Dorothea Brooke and Maggie Tulliver demonstrate two different alternatives to the positive self-image and the conventionally happy ending.

Chapter 3

IMAGES OF THE SELF:
THE NEGATIVE IMAGE

I am not sure that the greatest man of his age, if ever that
solitary superlative existed, could escape these unfavourable
reflections of himself in various small mirrors; and even
Milton, looking for his portrait in a spoon, must submit
to have the facial angle of a bumpkin. (M, 62)

George Eliot's complex vision of the problem of self-image is projected in
this passage from *Middlemarch*. Having related the various negative opinions
which Mrs. Cadwallader, Celia, Mr. Brooke and Sir James Chettam hold about
Mr. Casaubon, Eliot intrudes into the narrative--"I protest against any absolute conclusion" (M, 62) --and proceeds to argue for the relativity of self-
image. Using the mirror analogy, Eliot demonstrates how the scope and angle
of the medium of vision may affect the kind of image one receives of the
self. The "small mirrors," representing the clear but limited vision of the
Middlemarch characters, provide the gazer with a reflection which is superficially accurate but simplistic in its limited scope. The spoon itself is a distorted object, and the gazer who uses this medium will inevitably receive
a correspondingly distorted and illusory reflection.

There are, it is suggested, two main kinds of errors which may delude the character in search of a self-image. The first error is to mistake clarity for completeness and to ignore the problem of scope: to accept uncritically and to internalize the opinions of society without regard to the limitations of its provinciality. The second error consists in choosing an incorrect medium of reflection. The viewer who is deluded enough to trust a distorted medium will pay the price of her delusion in the distorted self-image which her chosen medium reflects.

Dorothea Brooke and Maggie Tulliver are talented heroines whose self-images illustrate the results of these errors. Maggie gazes into the "small mirror" of the Dodson values and accepts the image of herself as outcast and alien which she finds there. Dorothea, like Milton, searches for an unconventional medium of vision. She finds her "spoon" in Mr. Casaubon and all that he represents; her struggle consists in the attempt to wrench her personality into correspondence with the distorted image provided by the inaccurate medium she has chosen.

Because Maggie and Dorothea mistakenly trust' mediums of vision which are inherently lacking in scope and in clarity and because they internalize these distorted reflections, each of them suffers from a sense of the self as inadequate. Their self-images are negative in the sense that they represent self-defeating standards which threaten the heroines' self-esteem and sense of personal worth. The term "negative," as applied to the self-images of Maggie and Dorothea, is not meant to suggest that these heroines consistently think of themselves as morally evil human beings. They do have their moments of intense self-reproach but this is not unique to them; the heroines who have been described as possessing "positive" self-images also experience periods of self-criticism and self-condemnation.

The essential distinction between the positive and the negative self-image can best be described in terms of scope. Elizabeth Bennet's and Emma's self-images are illusory because they presuppose a largeness of scope which is beyond the power of even the most talented heroine. Such powers as omniscient perception, infallible judgement and the ability to manipulate others always for their own good are simply not available to those who share in the imperfect human condition. There is, however, a certain healthy quality in a self-image which assumes a larger scope. The ability to perceive oneself in terms of expansiveness, knowledge and control points to an assumption of self-confidence and a sense of self-esteem. When Emma and Elizabeth are disabused of their illusory notions about the self, the vastness of their imagined scope diminishes but the intensity of their existence as human beings is increased. This is an essentially healthy process, for it leads to self-knowledge and to a fulfilling existence within the human community.

Maggie and Dorothea experience a process which, in terms of self-image, is almost the reverse of Emma's and Elizabeth's. The Eliot heroines adopt self-images which are too narrow in scope and which thwart the full development of their personalities. Maggie internalizes the rigid, unimaginative expectations of her society and unsuccessfully attempts to fulfill these expectations. Her efforts to subdue her aspirations, intelligence and sensitivity are contrary to her own nature and these many failures in self-repression constantly reinforce her sense of alienation. Dorothea aspires to a large scope for action but she erroneously chooses the inhibiting standards of Mr. Casaubon as a means of achieving this scope. When she fails to meet his expectations, Dorothea develops a sense of herself as inadequate and inferior.

The negative self-image is one which is essentially alien to the heroine's integrity as a person and which is psychologically unhealthy because it can repress the vital human needs for self-assertion and self-fulfillment. The negative self-image is a kind of psychic imprisonment; but it is not necessarily a hopeless incarceration. The key to freedom lies in the critical examination of the visual medium: when one sees that the spoon is distorted, one no longer trusts the accuracy of its reflection. Dorothea's self-image evolves because she attains this critical perception of Mr. Casaubon. Maggie's self-image changes but never evolves into a positive one because she fails to free herself from the limited standards of her world: she remains lost in the labyrinth of a grotesque fun-house.

DOROTHEA BROOKE

When Miss Brooke is introduced in the first chapter of *Middlemarch* she seems
to be a young lady with a very strong sense of self-esteem. Her condescending
treatment of Celia over the matter of their mother's jewels reflects a "strong
assumption of superiority." (*M*, 9) Her blunt refusal of Sir James Chettam's
gallant offer of a riding horse demonstrates a great sense of herself as distinct
from other women. When Sir James urges "Every lady ought to be a perfect
horsewoman, that she may accompany her husband," Dorothea proudly
asserts her own unconventionality:

> *"You see how widely we differ, Sir James. I have made up
> my mind that I ought not to be a perfect horsewoman, and
> so I should never correspond to your pattern of a lady."
> Dorothea looked straight before her, and spoke with a cold
> brusquerie, very much with the air of a handsome boy, in
> amusing contrast with the solicitous amiability of her ad-
> mirer. (M, 16)*

The apparently positive, even superior, self-image which Dorothea seems to
display is not, however, a very strong one. Her treatment of Celia and Sir
James is really motivated by an intense and frustrated religious ardor. Since
Dorothea's situation provides no appropriate cause in whose service she can
expend her ardor, her devotion can be expressed only negatively through such
Puritanical trivialities as the disapproval of pretty jewels and the renunciation
of the legitimate pleasures of riding. Despite some superficial manifestations
of superiority, Dorothea has a sense of herself as ignorant and inadequately
educated which is shown in her efforts at self-instruction: the memorization
of passages from Pascal's *Pensees* and Jeremy Taylor's works. The apparently
learned Mr. Casaubon reinforces her image of herself as inadequate and lacking
fulfillment.

The real appeal which Casaubon holds for Dorothea is that he appears to
possess the kind of knowledge which will enable her to attain self-fulfillment.
She is delighted by the opportunity to aid Casaubon in his "great works"
but her meditation reveals an equally eager desire to use the knowledge which
Casaubon will provide to further her own personal schemes:

> *"I should learn everything then . . . It would be my duty to*

study that I might help him the better in his great works . . .
It would be like marrying Pascal. I should learn to see the
truth by the same light as great men have seen it by. And
then I should know what to do when I get older: I should
see how it was possible to lead a grand life here--now--in
England. I don't feel sure about doing good in any way now:
. . . unless it were building good cottages--there can be no
doubt about that. Oh, I hope I should be able to get people
well housed in Lowick! I will draw plenty of plans when
I have time." (M, 21)

There is a great deal of illusion in Dorothea's optimistic plans. She unconsciously assumes that Casaubon's aspirations will coincide with her own. There is also an unconscious egoism inherent in her scheme. All unknowingly, Dorothea looks to the intellectually and emotionally sterile pedant as an udder to feed her supreme self. (*M*, 156)

Dorothea's feelings about herself undergo an evolution during her honeymoon in Rome. Her former image of herself as an ignorant aspirant for knowledge is replaced by a more negative image of herself as personally, as well as intellectually, inadequate. She has a profound sense of having disappointed Mr. Casaubon and her efforts to help him in his work paradoxically exacerbate him. Dorothea still has illusions about Casaubon's superiority which prevent her from criticizing his cold, insensitive behavior. Instead, she blames herself, although she in ignorant of the nature of her offense:

> *Yet Dorothea had no distinctly shapen grievance that she*
> *could state even to herself; and in the midst of her confused*
> *thought and passion, the mental act that was struggling forth*
> *into clearness was a self-accusing cry that her feeling of*
> *desolation was the fault of her own spiritual poverty. (M,*
> *143)*

Dorothea's "offense" has been a failure to meet Casaubon's expectations. He had hoped for a young bride who would observe "his abundant pen-scratches and amplitude of paper with the uncritical awe of an elegant-minded canary-bird." (*M*, 149) Instead, he finds he has married an intellectually acute woman, eager for knowledge, and critical of the slow pace of his work. Dorothea is of course unaware that Casaubon's great insecurity and defensiveness arise from his proud fear that his "vast knowledge" will be exposed as the pedantic maze of unrelated scraps which it really is.

When Will Ladislaw disabuses Dorothea of her illusions about the worth of Casaubon's research, he provides the occasion for a great growth in self-knowledge on Dorothea's part. Her moral sensitivity is touched when she thinks how the labor of her husband's life might be in vain. Her early self-image of herself as the unfulfilled aspirant is replaced by the realization that Mr. Casaubon is the one who is truly unfulfilled and that he is incapable of helping her realize her own ardent aspirations:

> *Today she had begun to see that she had been under a wild illusion in expecting a response to her feeling from Mr. Casaubon, and she had felt the waking of a presentiment that there might be a sad consciousness in his life which made as great a need on his side as on her own.*

> *We are all of us born in moral stupidity, taking the world as an udder to feed our supreme selves. Dorothea had early begun to emerge from that stupidity, but yet it had been easier for her to imagine how she would devote herself to Mr. Casaubon, and become wise and strong in his strength and wisdom, than to conceive with that distinctness which is no longer reflection but feeling . . . that he had an equivalent centre of self, whence the lights and shadows must always fall with a certain difference. (M, 156-157)*

When Dorothea returns to Lowick, her blue-green boudoir, like her own self-image, seems to have diminished in size, vividness, and reality--it is a ghostly blue-green world. As she considers the disappointments which her married life has brought, she confronts the reality that the "active wifely devotion which was to strengthen her husband's life and exalt her own" (M, 202) will probably never materialize. She feels acutely the moral imprisonment of the situation to which her illusory self-image has led her. Since she can no longer revere her husband, she resolves to turn to duty as a source of inspiration for her married life.

Dorothea does fulfill her duty for the rest of her married life: rising in the night to read, ever solicitous of her husband's health, unwilling to upset or agitate him, Dorothea pities Casaubon's failure and sees her proper role to be one of offering consolation.

> *She was no longer struggling against the perception of facts, but adjusting herself to their clearest perception; and now*

*when she looked steadily at her husband's failure, still more
at his possible consciousness of failure, she seemed to be
looking along the one track where duty became tenderness.*
(M, 267)

By defining herself solely in terms of her husband's needs, Dorothea virtually
annihilates her own sense of herself as a person. Her marital duties suppress
her formerly active and aspiring social consciousness. When Lydgate tells her
about his problems with the new hospital, her reply reveals the limitations of
her existence:

*"I shall be quite grateful to you if you will tell me how I can
help to make things a little better. Everything of that sort has
slipped away from me since I have been married." (M, 320)*

Her marriage is a "perpetual struggle of energy with fear." (M, 285) Dorothea's
energy manifests itself in the occasional moments of rebellion which come to
her in the privacy of her boudoir. Here she indulges in periods of angry self-
assertion as she struggles to maintain some sense of her own individuality, to
gather together the remnants of her shattered self-esteem. In one of these
moments she bitterly reflects:

*Was it her fault that she had believed in him--had believed in
his worthiness? --And what, exactly was he? --She was able
enough to estimate him--she who waited on his glances with
trembling, and shut her best soul in prison, paying it only
hidden visits, that she might be petty enough to please
him. (M, 313)*

Because of her fear for her husband's health, however, Dorothea never confronts Casaubon with her grievances. She is denied the healthy release of self-
expression and must struggle in silence until she represses her anger and can
once more assume a submissive stance.

Perhaps the clearest instance of Dorothea's loss of her sense of selfhood and
personal integrity occurs when she decides to submit to Casaubon's "dead
hand." Casaubon's desire to bind his young wife to a long widowhood among
the fragments of the worthless Key to all Mythologies represents the ultimate
egoism. Dorothea has trained herself in submission and self-repression and her
ultimate self-effacement is her willingness to define herself forever as Casaubon's widow and to subdue her aspirations and intellect to the task of:

. . . sorting what might be called shattered mummies and

51

fragments of a tradition which was itself a mosaic wrought
from crushed ruins--sorting them as food for a theory which
was already withered in the birth like an elfin child. (M, 351)

Casaubon's "dead hand" is ironically the very means by which Dorothea regains her sense of self-esteem. On a literal level, Casaubon frees her from the imprisonment of the Key because he dies before she has given her promise. On another level, his egoistic desire to control her life by the codicil to his will which would deprive her of her property if she should marry Will Ladislaw frees her from all her emotional ties to Casaubon's memory. Dorothea realizes that she has never really known the man whom she so dutifully served and for whom she so completely abnegated herself. The codicil is the final insult to her integrity which frees Dorothea from Casaubon's cold grasp:

> *The grasp had slipped away. Bound by a pledge given from*
> *the depths of her pity, she [Dorothea] would have been*
> *capable of undertaking a toil which her judgment whispered*
> *was vain for all uses except that consecration of faithfulness*
> *which is a supreme use. But now her judgment, instead*
> *of being controlled by duteous devotion, was made active*
> *by the imbittering discovery that in her past union there had*
> *lurked the hidden alienation of secrecy and suspicion. The*
> *living, suffering man was no longer before her to awaken her*
> *pity: there remained only the retrospect of painful subjec-*
> *tion to a husband whose thoughts had been lower than she*
> *had believed . . .* (M, 362)

At last Dorothea realizes the perversity of the man whose expectations she had striven unsuccessfully to fulfill and whose standards had led her to judge herself as ignorant, unfulfilled, and personally insignificant. Her own self-image had been distorted by the egoism of the medium which she had so naively trusted and whose negative reflections she had so uncritically internalized.

Dorothea's mature self-image is a benevolent, humanistic one. She no longer sees herself as an inadequate being who depends upon the resources of others for self-fulfillment. Rather, Dorothea views herself as a strong member of the human family who is capable of giving and of helping others to attain self-fulfillment. She concerns herself with the problem of filling the Lowick living and enriches the life of the Farebrother family through her decision. She strengthens Lydgate by believing in his innocence when all of society suspects or condemns him. Overcoming her personal agony, she visits Rosamund to offer courage and to "save" Rosamund from what Dorothea imagines to be a self-destructive adulterous relationship with Will.

Dorothea's story, unlike Elizabeth's, Emma's and Jane Eyre's, does not close with a perfect marriage. Dorothea's marriage to Will is not "ideally beautiful" (M, 612) and the great aspirations of her youth are never fulfilled. Her very willingness to marry Will, however, shows the strength of her self-image. Dorothea is confident enough to risk vulnerability by marrying a man whose potential is as yet unrealized. Her belief that she can make Will happy shows the strength of her image of herself as one who has much to give. Indeed, the *Finale* to *Middlemarch* stresses the fullness of Dorothea's nature by invoking a comparison between her strength and that of a mighty river:

> *Her full nature, like that river of which Cyrus broke the strength, spent itself in channels which had no great name on the earth. But the effect of her being on those around her was incalculably diffusive . . . (M, 613)*

MAGGIE TULLIVER

River imagery plays an even greater and more significant role in defining the nature of Maggie Tulliver, another of Eliot's heroines. Maggie spends her childhood at Dorlcote Mill, located on a tributary of the river Floss. Maggie's destiny is linked to the course of this river which, appropriately, is described as possessing almost human characteristics. *The Mill on the Floss* opens with this account of the river Floss:

> *A wide plain, where the broadening Floss hurries on between its green banks to the sea, and the loving tide, rushing to meet it, checks its passage with an impetuous embrace. (MF, 7)*

The Floss, like Maggie herself, is impulsive and passionate. It hurries to meet the "loving" tide as one lover rushes to another; and the river and tide meet with an "impetuous embrace." When Maggie yields to her passionate nature she is, significantly, drifting languorously along this very river and she later meets her death in the grip of its "impetuous embrace."

The river Floss functions throughout the novel to define the loving, ardent and spontaneous aspects of Maggie's nature. While the river is not an image of Maggie's self, but an image which George Eliot creates for the reader, it does act as a kind of objective correlative for Maggie's self-image. Maggie images herself in various ways--as an outcast and alien, as an ascetic--but her predominant image is of herself as a child. The river Floss represents the emotional content of her childhood to Maggie: her desperate love for her brother Tom, her beloved father's unhappy fate, and her family's claim to her own fidelity and devotion. When, at the end of the novel, Maggie drifts along the Floss--"borne along by the tide" of her passion for Stephen Guest--she dreams of the river and returns to her childhood in her dream:

> *She was in a boat on the wide water with Stephen, and in the gathering darkness something like a star appeared, that grew and grew till they saw it was the Virgin seated in St. Ogg's boat, and it came nearer and nearer, till they saw the Virgin was Lucy and the boatman was Philip--no, not Philip, but her brother, who rowed past without looking at her; and she rose to stretch out her arms and call to him, and their own boat turned over with the movement, and they began to sink, till with one spasm of dread, she seemed to awake, and find that she was a child again in the parlour at evening twilight, and Tom was not really angry.* (MF, 412-413)

Maggie's dream reveals much about her own self-image. Her idealization of Lucy and her sense of inferiority to Lucy cause her to transform Lucy into the Virgin Mary. Through this transformation Maggie bestows upon Lucy the attributes of purity and sinlessness traditionally associated with the Virgin. As an awkward, unattractive little girl, Maggie had imagined the perfect Lucy to be a diminutive fairy queen "with a little crown on her head and a little sceptre in her hand." (MF, 55) Now Maggie is a grown woman suffering from a sense of moral inferiority to her cousin.

In her dream, Maggie momentarily confuses her brother Tom with Philip Wakem. Each of them embodies expectations which she had tried to fulfill in her past. Philip, her adolescent mentor, had urged Maggie to be true to her own nature, and had prophetically warned her of the dangers of self-repression:

> *"You will be thrown into the world some day, and then every rational satisfaction of your nature that you deny now, will assault you like a savage appetite."* (MF, 288)

Now that Philip's prediction is being fulfilled, Maggie subconsciously realizes the accuracy of his perception and she momentarily canonizes him by transforming him into St. Ogg.

The image of Philip is, however, quickly effaced by the image of her brother Tom. Tom and Philip, so unlike in every way, merge in Maggie's unconsciousness because they are the two whose love she has cherished and who have defined contradictory standards for her. Tom's image replaces Philip's because his influence has been the strongest one in Maggie's life. Tom's love and esteem were the great needs of her childhood and Tom's displeasure, always followed by a withdrawal of his love, provoked the greatest crises of Maggie's youth. Tom, like Philip, has been a mentor and moral guide for Maggie and his standards have been the very opposite of Philip's. While Philip urged self-fulfillment, Tom demanded self-repression. Philip's respect for the imagination was countered by Tom's stolid common sense and his suspicion of anything intangible. Philip's trust in the essential goodness of Maggie's nature was clearly at odds with Tom's critical view of Maggie's impetuousity and emotionality:

> "You're always in extremes--you have no judgment and self-command" (MF, 342) . . . "I never feel certain of anything with you. At one time you take pleasure in a sort of perverse self-denial, and at another you have not resolution to resist a thing you know to be wrong." (MF, 343)

Tom's judgment, like Philip's prophecy, is in the process of being vindicated. While dreaming, Maggie is literally in a boat with Lucy's unofficial fiance, and her yielding to Stephen's influence has indeed come about because she had not resisted what she knew to be wrong. In Maggie's dream Tom rejects her, as he had so often in real life, and the result of his rejection is a terrible one. When she was a child, Tom's rejections had plunged Maggie into paroxysms of self-destructive despair. Now, in her dream, his rejection causes her total destruction: the boat turns over and she begins to sink. The only thing which can save her from death is a return to her childhood state. The great reward of returning to the parlor at home is the renewal of Tom's love; she finds that Tom "was not really angry."

Maggie's dream both summarizes the struggle of her past and predicts her future end. Her inability to fulfill the Dodson standards, which were personified in Tom, caused the young Maggie to see herself as rejected and alien. As a grown woman, Maggie has intellectually rebelled against these standards while she emotionally retains them. Self-control, self-discipline, practicality, material-ism, duty, the predominance of justice over mercy: these are the Dodson standards which Maggie has internalized. In her period of asceticism, she seemed to have compelled her spirit into obedience to these expectations. During her relationship with Philip, when her budding sexuality and emotional nature threatened her adherence to these principles, she took refuge in the a-sexual mental image of herself as a child. This defense worked against Philip, but it failed her in her infatuation with Stephen. In succumbing to Stephen's charm, Maggie loses her sense of selfhood, just as Dorothea did in her willing-ness to yield to Casaubon's "dead hand." After she has so egregiously violated the Dodson code, Maggie perceives only one source of refuge. Never having learned that "you can't go home again," she runs back to Tom, only to meet with his cruelest and most final rejction. In her death, Maggie finds peace because her unconscious self-image becomes a reality. She and Tom return to the state of childhood:

> . . . *brother and sister had gone down in an embrace never to be parted: living again in one supreme moment, the days when they had clasped their little hands in love, and roamed the daisied fields together.* (MF, 456)

The ending of *The Mill on the Floss* has been criticized from many perspec-tives. One of the most common focuses of criticism has been the alleged sentimentality of the novel's resolution. It has been pointed out, for example, that Tom and Maggie's childhood relationship rarely approached the idyllic state which the concluding passage describes. It is true that we seem to remem-ber the scenes of discord between brother and sister more vividly than those moments when they "clasped their little hands in love."

In terms of Maggie's self-image, however, the rhetoric of the ending is singu-larly appropriate. What the mature Maggie remembers of her childhood is the idealized state of loving and of being loved. The desire to relive this childhood memory, to fuse past and present, leads her to Tom through the surging waters of the terrible flood. Of course Maggie's recollection of her childhood is partly illusory; it is a creation of the needs of her own illusory self-image. The resolu-tion of *The Mill on the Floss*, in its treatment of Tom's and Maggie's "fulfill-ment" is surely every bit as tempered as the ending of *Middlemarch*. Maggie's aspirations are not realized; her loving personality is never fulfilled. She moves, in the novel, from childhood to childhood; her self-image varies from one of the rejected child to the self as a child. The movement of the novel, as far as

Maggie's self-image is concerned, is not progressive or evolving; it is essentially circular. Hence it is not impossible to see in the ending of *The Mill on the Floss* a muted, ironic commentary upon Maggie's failure to attain maturity and her persistently illusory view of herself.

In considering the self-images of the other talented heroines it has been necessary, as it were, to begin at the beginning. It would be extremely difficult, for example, to discuss Dorothea's self-image intelligently by reference to a passage from the end of *Middlemarch*. This is so because of the progressively evolving nature of Dorothea's self-image. Her essentially negative self-image gradually gives way to a positive sense of herself as strong and as capable of giving. Maggie's negative self-image, however, is never replaced by a positive one. Unlike Dorothea, she never rejects the source of her self-image but continues to assess herself according to the reflection of the small mirrors of her family and her world.

As a child, Maggie consistently sees herself as an outcast and an ailen. She cannot be like the pretty, lifeless Lucy, who epitomizes the Dodson standards for little girls. Maggie is incapable of appearing ornamentally neat and tidy, her hair refuses to curl as it should, her skin is unpleasantly brown: she is not a possession of which her mother can be proud. Mrs. Tulliver, in the best Calvinistic sense, interprets Maggie's unconventionality as a judgment upon herself. After Maggie has vindictively ruined her curls by soaking her hair, Mrs. Tulliver remonstrates:

> "I'll tell your aunt Glegg and your aunt Pullet when they
> come next week, and they'll never love you any more. Oh
> dear, Oh dear! look at your clean pinafore, wet from top to
> bottom. Folks 'ull think it's a judgment on me as I've got
> such a child--they'll think I've done summat wicked."
> (MF, 25)

In the best Dodson sense, Mrs. Tulliver is concerned with externals and possessions. Maggie is not a possession which she can display with the pride with which Mrs. Deane exhibits Lucy. Unconventional children, like rough hair and dirty pinafores, are undesirable reflections on oneself; for material prosperity is a sign of God's favor, according to the secular calvinism of the Dodsons. Love, too, is a commodity, useful for bargaining, to be bestowed or retracted according to the whim of the giver. Tom, even as a child, illustrates the Dodson conception of love. When Maggie lets his rabbits die, his retaliation is the withdrawal of love: "And I don't love you, Maggie. You shan't go fishing with me to-morrow. I told you to go and see the rabbits every day." (*MF*, 32)

"I don't love you": these are the words which can collapse Maggie's small world in an instant. After her mother's threat and after Tom's rejection, Maggie's reaction is the same. She retreats to the attic where her physical isolation is emblematic of the alienation she feels. There she has a wooden doll which is a kind of fetish and which provides her with a way of expressing her anger and frustration. Maggie makes the doll her victim and sees it as another self. The acute pain which Maggie feels is expressed in her abusive treatment of her doll. The victimized doll, "defaced by a long career of vicarious suffering" (*MF*, 26) is really a projection of Maggie's own self-image.

Perhaps the incident which is most illustrative of Maggie's self-image is her flight to the gypsy camp. Maggie has aroused Tom's anger by causing him to do a most un-Dodson-like thing. In her impetuous excitement over Uncle Pullet's musical snuff-box, Maggie causes Tom to spill half of his wine. No Dodson likes to look careless or undignified, least of all Tom, and he punishes Maggie by ignoring her and paying excessive attention to the perfect little Lucy. Maggie's jealousy is acute but the blow which pushes poor Lucy into the mud is provoked by Tom's rejection: "Now, get away, Maggie. There's no room for you on the grass here. Nobody asked *you* to come." (*MF*, 90)

Tom has labeled her an outcast and Maggie determines to flee to the gypsies who are, like herself, alienated from respectable society. Maggie's action shows the extent to which she has internalized the criticisms of the Dodson clan. They have often enough reminded Maggie of her brown skin, her wildness, and her general resemblance to a gypsy. George Eliot calls Maggie's escape to the gypsy camp a flight "from her own shadow." Indeed, Maggie is fleeing from herself. She is leaving a self which has been rejected and deprecated for a world where she hopes to be accepted and honored "on account of her superior knowledge." (*MF*, 94) Of course, the gypsies care little for her superior knowledge, but the incident is illustrative of Maggie's respect for learning and of her desire to be considered clever since she cannot satisfy the Dodson standards for prettiness.

Maggie's desire to escape her shadow finds another avenue of expression when she enters early womanhood. Seeking an explanation of the "hard, real life" to which her father's bankruptcy has exposed her, Maggie embraces the doctrine of renunciation set forth in Thomas a Kempis' *Imitation of Christ*. Maggie is struggling with herself in attempting to suppress her rebellion at the loveless, joyless, lot which is now hers:

> *She wanted some explanation of this hard, real life: the unhappy-looking father, seated at the dull breakfast-table; the childish, bewildered mother; the little sordid tasks that filled the hours, or the more oppressive emptiness of weary, joyless leisure; the need of some tender, demonstrative love; the cruel sense that Tom didn't mind what she thought or felt, and that they were no longer playfellows together. . .* (MF, 251)

Like Dorothea, Maggie imagines that some key exists which will render all sorrow explicable and endurable; she thinks she has found her key in the *Imitation* and her identity by embracing the image of herself as an ascetic. Maggie's new self-image is illustrated by her mirror which she hangs with its face to the wall. In refusing to look at herself, Maggie attempts to annihilate her sense of selfhood just as Dorothea did by repressing herself in order to please Mr. Casaubon. Maggie's superficial asceticism, however, resembles more closely the puritanical self-denial of the young Dorothea. Maggie's asceticism is immature because it does not diminish her self-absorption but simply redirects it. She is consumed with interest as she watches herself play out the drama of asceticism:

> *From what you know of her, you will not be surprised that she threw some exaggeration and wilfulness, some pride and impetuousity into her self-renunciation: her own life was still a drama for her, in which she demanded of herself that her part should be played with intensity.* (MF, 256)

When Philip Wakem threatens Maggie's ascetic image of herself by tempting her with books, music and, most of all, love, Maggie reacts by denying her femininity and by seeing herself as a child. Her unconscious defense against her own sensuality and the obvious sexual attraction which she holds for Philip is to freeze their relationship into the one which they had enjoyed as children:

> *The idea that he [Philip] might become her lover . . . had not occurred to her; and Philip saw the absence of this idea clearly enough-- . . . There was bitterness to him in the*

clearly enough-- . . . There was bitterness to him in the
perception that Maggie was almost as frank and unconstrained
towards him as when she was a child. (MF, 265)

In her relationship with Philip, Maggie's ascetic image merges with her image of herself as a child. When Philip criticizes the "dead level" of their provincial existence, Maggie suppresses her discontent by reasoning:

"But, dear Philip, I think we are only like children, that
some one who is wiser is taking care of. Is it not right to
resign ourselves entirely, whatever may be denied us?" (MF,
286)

Maggie clings to this image of herself as a child because she is unwilling to face the crises which adult sexuality engenders. After her first physical contact with Stephen when she takes his arm in the garden, Maggie immediately wishes, "Oh, Philip, Philip, I wish we were together again--so quietly--in the Red Deeps." (*MF*, 357) Philip represents the peace and tranquility of the child's innocent, unconscious sexuality; he becomes Maggie's mental refuge from the turbulence of her sexually charged relationship with Stephen.

Essentially, however, Maggie persists in seeing herself as a child because it is the only level upon which she can still relate to Tom. Tom will guide, direct, and chastise her, but he will not enter into a relationship of equality with her. Although she rebels intellectually, Maggie is so emotionally dependent upon Tom's approval that she approaches him with all the diffidence of an obedient child and asks his permission to see Philip again.

It is part of Maggie's tragedy that she never develops the maturity to reject Tom's values. After she has performed the most morally sensitive act of her life by leaving Stephen, she makes the great mistake of turning to Tom as her "natural refuge." (*MF*, 423)[1] Maggie's heroic act of love and fidelity to her past, to Philip, and to Lucy impresses Tom as merely a disgrace. Tom sees only as the "world's wife" sees: he judges according to results, lacking the moral sensitivity to imagine the mental suffering by which these results are arrived at. When Tom turns Maggie from his door he stands for all of St. Ogg society. The cycle is complete: Maggie is once again the alien, the outcast, the rejected child.

The consideration of the problem of self-image points to the reciprocity which exists between the self and society. In one sense, the talented heroines create what they see. That is, they see their societies in a way which reflects the images which they have created of themselves. But the self-images of the heroines are not formed in a vacuum. Indeed, we have seen how they may internalize the standards of their societies in forming their own self-images. The struggles of Dorothea and Maggie illustrate the negative effects which the uncritical internalizing of others' opinions can have upon the talented heroine. The difference between the fates of these two heroines points also to the responsibility of the heroine for the state of her own self-image. Dorothea could have remained forever imprisoned by the inadequate self-image which she ingested from Mr. Casaubon. Her own intellectual acuity, however, was her salvation. Maggie's emotional, unreflecting nature prevents her from critically examining the Dodson values. Her tragedy is as much a result of her immaturity as it is a product of her society's provinciality.

If one were to extract from the novels all of the various facts about the five heroines--birth, appearance, family life, education, occupation, etc.--and arrange this data according to the impersonal format of a case study, surely the social worker or psychologist would judge that the heroine with the most negative self-image must be Jane Eyre. An orphaned child, plain and homely, subjected to harassment and humiliation at "home" and school, occupying the demeaning social position of governess, Jane would seem to have no source for a sense of self-esteem and personal worth. Yet it has been demonstrated that she possesses the most positive and least illusory self-image of all the heroines. Jane's self-esteem, and that of the other heroines, is intimately related to her self-definition. The conscious role that each heroine adopts in her society, her self-definition, must be considered in assessing the problems which the unconventional, talented heroine encounters in forming her sense of self.

Chapter 4

SELF AND SOCIETY:
THE PROBLEM OF SELF—DEFINITION

In *The Philosophy of Existentialism* Gabriel Marcel discusses the depersonalization of modern humanity in a post-industrial society. The contemporary
pragmatic preoccupation with material values has led, Marcel believes, to a
misplacement of the idea of function. The individual in today's society has lost
the awareness of the self as being and tends to appear as a mere agglomeration
of functions. Modern persons, in losing the ontological sense of being, have
come to define themselves solely in terms of their various functions: as con-
sumers, producers, citizens, etc. The dehumanizing effect of this modern
functionalised world is evidenced in the loss of a sense of selfhood. For example, the subway employee who defines himself in terms of his role as ticket-
puncher experiences an alienation from his true inner being and feels the "dull,
intolerable unease" of an actor who is reduced to living as though he were in
fact submerged by his role or function.[1]

The dehumanizing, depersonalizing effects of what Marcel calls a "functionalised world" are perhaps more dramatically displayed in modern times because
we live in a highly industrialized, technological and computerized society.
The ticket puncher's plight is vivid to us because we can picture him perform-
ing his mechanized task amidst the sea of blank-faced commuters absorbing the
impersonal stock-market statistics which chart industrial progress or decline.
But the problem of "functionalism," while more striking in our century, is not
unique to our time.[2] Nor is the tendency to define oneself solely in terms of
one's function always directly linked to industrialism. It is easy enough to see
in the nineteenth century mills and sweat-shops the beginnings of the modern

62

person's alienation from his inner self. Dickens' Wemmick from *Great Expectations* is a fictional precursor of the modern commuter's schizoid pattern of living. Not so readily apparent, however, is the fact that "functionalism's" effects were not limited in the nineteenth century to those many middle and lower-class men and lower-class women who ventured forth to earn their living amidst the "dark Satanic mills."[3]

The interest in women's role which this century has witnessed has sparked an awareness of the way in which those who do not participate directly in the business of the outside world can be similarly depersonalized by the identification of themselves with their functions. Betty Friedan's relatively early study (1963) *The Feminine Mystique* did much to illustrate how the neuroses, conflicts and dissatisfactions of contemporary middle-class women stem from the housewife's complete identification of herself with her social role. The depersonalizing effects of filling the roles of "someone's wife" and "someone's mother" can be seen in the unconsciously derogatory way in which many of these dissatisfied women verbally define themselves: "I'm only a housewife."

Since Friedan's study appeared scores of more sophisticated and scholarly works have urged married women to seek self-fulfillment, often through joining the labor force, and have enjoined upon single working women the necessity to struggle for equal rights and privileges with their male co-workers. The Women's Liberation Movement of our century has produced a strangely mixed progeny: some of its fruits are applauded by almost all fair-minded persons while the eccentricity of some of its other products has been met with laughter, scorn and bemusement. Some critics of the women's movement, for example, consider the current trend for married women to keep their maiden names to be an example of the latter. This desire to retain one's own name in preference to assuming the name, and implicitly, the identity of another person is interesting in terms of this study because it points to the way in which self-image and self-definition are related. The contemporary married woman who aspires to regain a sense of her own being, as distinct from her functions, attempts to create an image of herself as an independent, complete human person who chooses to perform certain wifely and motherly tasks. This self-image is in a sense contradicted by assuming another's name for, from Biblical times, the conferring of a name signifies the superiority of the one who does the bestowing. Hence, it is easy to see how defining oneself to the outward world in terms of another person's name and identity can conflict with the interior image of the woman as a complete person in her own right.

Like many women today, each of the talented heroines strives to attain a self-image which reflects her unique personality. The heroines find that the stereotyped self-definitions which their societies attempt to impose upon them often conflict with their desires for personal freedom. It has been noted, for example, how the ornamental and essentially useless education of middle-class young women was geared to one end--the attainment of a husband--and how the lonely fate of the old maid was to be avoided at all costs. Dr. Gregory, in effect, urged his daughters to suppress all signs of their own identity--health, wit, learning, etc.--in order that they might one day achieve the reward of defining themselves as wives.

The society of middle-class England in the last century was, in truth, every bit as "functionalised" as the contemporary society which Marcel criticizes. Women, in particular, were seen chiefly in terms of their roles or functions as daughters, wives, and mothers. Today we recognize how role playing is one way in which the individual can relate to her society:

> *An individual's social position is intimately related to pat-*
> *tern's of action--to the way others behave toward [her] and*
> *the behavior expected of [her]--what social scientists call*
> *"roles."* [4]

The fulfillment of certain social roles should not, in itself, necessarily be considered as limited or repressive. Contemporary society still commands the fulfillment of roles but, unlike the society of the last century, allows for a greater diversity of roles and a larger degree of freedom of individual choice. From our perspective today, however, we can recognize the severe limitations of certain roles, especially the extremely rigid and small repertory of roles available to the woman of the last century. The prolific writings of Mrs. Sarah Ellis illustrate this point. The titles of the works in her *Women of England* series exhaust the options for self-definition available to the middle-class young lady: *Daughters of England* (1843) *Wives of England* (1843) and *Mothers of England* (1845). If a woman were so unfortunate as never to progress beyond the first step of "daughter" to the exalted level of "wife" she was, nevertheless, defined in these same terms. Society defined the unmarried woman by ne-gation, she was the woman without a husband, and as long as her parents lived she was defined by her role as daughter. The complaint of one spinster in 1868 illustrates this fact:

> *"The position of a single woman of thirty in the middle-*

*classes is horrible. Her cares are to be properly dressed, to
drive or walk or pay calls with Mamma; to work miracles of
embroidery--but for what? What we want is something to
do, something to live for."*[5]

Daughter, wife, mother: these are limited options indeed. The smallness of
scope provided by these alternatives is further underscored when one considers
how each of them offers an opportunity for self-definition only in terms of
another person's existence. The typical girl of the last century exchanged her
father's authority and identity for her husband's; her society expected her to
perform the role of the potential wife while still a daughter, and to fulfill her
role as mother by forming her female children into potentially desirable wives.
The lack of a sense of personal identity which resulted from the nineteenth
century's "functionalised" view of women has been succinctly stated by Zea
Zinn:

> *The assumption on which the concept of the female charac-
> ter was based was . . . that women existed not for themselves
> nor for whatever contribution to society they as individuals
> could make, but for the pleasure and service they could
> render to men. It is important that we become aware of the
> corollaries to this doctrine. First, woman was dependent on
> man for her religious beliefs and her views on morals. There
> could be no difficulty about her ideas on other matters, for
> a woman had no mind of her own and should hold no views
> except those relating to her own duties. Her supreme duty
> was obedience, as a daughter to her parents, as a wife to her
> husband.*[6]

There were doubtlessly many women who unquestioningly and unreflectively
lived out the stereotyped cycle of society's expectations. In fiction, too,
numerous female characters willingly exchange the functions of daughter and
potential wife for the functions of wifehood and motherhood. Charlotte Lucas,
in *Pride and Prejudice*, swiftly acts to relieve her family's apprehensions of her
dying an old maid by accepting the proposal of the irksome Mr. Collins. The
obedient and submissive Lucy Deane in *The Mill on the Floss* weaves a lovely,
illusory romance around her expected marriage to Stephen Guest while the
socially ambitious Rosamund Vincy in *Middlemarch* rejoices at the opportunity to exchange her old self-definition as a manufacturer's daughter for the

more prestigious one of wife to the nephew of a baronet.

For the talented heroines, however, achieving self-definition is not simply a matter of acting pragmatically, like Charlotte Lucas, or romantically, like Lucy Deane, or ambitiously like Rosamund Vincy. Part of the dilemma of the talented heroine lies in the fact that the roles which society allows her to play are too limited for her to accept with the equanimity which the conventional heroines display. If, like Elizabeth Bennet, Jane Eyre and Dorothea, she refuses to fulfill society's expectations, the talented heroine may expect censure, ridicule and ostracism. If she attempts to disguise or suppress her aspirations, intelligence and sensitivity, as Emma and Maggie do, in order to fulfill stereo-typed social roles, she will inevitably damage her own unique personality. Mr. Deane states the dilemma succinctly in *The Mill on the Floss*: "If you want to slip into a round hole, you must make a ball of yourself--that's where it is." (*MF*, 203) The social dilemma of the talented heroine appears to be a most undesirable one: she must either remain at odds with society, or distort her personality--"make a ball" of herself--in order to fit comfortably into the social mold. The latter course is an obviously unsatisfactory one because, while it offers the heroine a socially acceptable self-definition, it simultaneously represses and effaces that unique self which was initially struggling to attain an appropriate sense of selfhood. One of the challenges which confronts the talented heroine is the task of achieving a kind of social poise which will enable her to operate within society while still remaining true to her own best self.

The problem of self-definition, of consciously choosing the role or stance one should adopt vis a vis one's society, begins in childhood. The family as the most basic social unit automatically afforded the nineteenth century girl the definition of herself as a dutiful, submissive daughter. All sorts of duties traditionally accrued to the function of being a daughter: obedience to one's father, respect for one's mother, deference towards one's brothers, and uncrit-ical loving affection for one's sisters.

In *The Women of England* Mrs. Sarah Stickney Ellis instructs the "daughters of England" in the duties of their functions in life. Young ladies are urged to regard their mothers with deference and to behave in an essentially subordinate manner:

> *It is true, the mother may be far behind the daughter in the accomplishments of modern education; she may, perhaps,*

occasionally betray her ignorance of polite literature, or her
want of acquaintance with the customs of polished society.
But how can this in any way affect the debt of obligation
existing between her daughter and herself? or how can it
lessen the validity of her claim to gratitude for services
received, and esteem for the faithfulness with which these
services have been performed?[7]

Towards their fathers, young women are urged to dare to be "dutiful daughters rather than ladies of fashion" and the principles of "integrity, generosity and natural feeling" should teach them "never to wish for enjoyment purchased by the sacrifice of a father's health, or a husband's peace."[8]

Sisters are to exhibit an unvarying affection towards one another and to be a constant source of consolation to each other:

They know each other's faults, but they behold them only to
pity and forgive, or speak of them only to correct . . . Each
has her own store of painful experience to unfold, and she
weeps to find her sister's greater than her own . . . Self
becomes as nothing in comparison with the intense interest
excited by a sister's experience . . .[9]

Finally, young women are to act as moral norms for their brothers, while remaining ever conscious of their own inferiority. If a sister has had to reproach her brother for some moral flaw, she must make restitution in the following manner:

In a gentle and unobtrusive manner, she does some extra
service for her brother, choosing what would otherwise be
degrading in its own nature, in order to prove in the most
delicate manner, that though she can see a fault in him, she
still esteems herself his inferior . . . In her intercourse with
men, it is impossible but that woman should feel her own
inferiority; and it is right that it should be so.[10]

Mrs. Ellis's advice suggests that an idyllic, untroubled family existence will be the happy result of a daughter's faithful fulfillment of her functions. She does not consider the complexities of family life which confront the talented heroines in their searches for self-definition. What if, as in the case of Elizabeth

Bennet, a daughter's acute perception prevents her from esteeming a mother who is essentially unworthy of respect or from cherishing a sister like Lydia? How can a girl like Maggie Tulliver, with her intellectual superiority to her brother Tom, be content to esteem herself his inferior? Mrs. Ellis does not inquire into such complexities but one suspects that if she did her advice would be "to suffer and be still." It is part of the dilemma of the talented heroine that, while she often suffers, she can rarely "be still." Because of their intelligence, aspirations and moral sensitivity the talented heroines are forced either to reject the subservient role which Mrs. Ellis describes or, if they do accept it, they often suffer the loss of their own identities.

The talented heroines are in various ways and for various reasons denied the easy sense of self-definition which the role of daughter traditionally offered. Jane Eyre and Dorothea are orphans and we do not see them in relation to their parents. Emma Woodhouse has only a father, who is selfish, senile and self-absorbed. Elizabeth Bennet and Maggie Tulliver possess both a mother and a father but the ineffectuality and impercipience of the Bennets and the Tullivers virtually negates them as powerful role models for their daughters.

It is significant that all five heroines either lack parents or possess only ineffectual ones. The absence of strong and dominant parental figures increases the heroines' freedom to define themselves and intensifies the degree of their moral responsibility. The fact that Emma, for example, defines herself in terms of her role as daughter is important because it is a freely chosen role. Similarly, Elizabeth Bennet's freedom to reject the social standards of her parents allows her to define herself according to her own personal moral values.

Because of the absence of parental domination, the heroines enjoy considerable freedom to accept or reject the expectations of their familial society. In terms of the larger society of their worlds, however, they are more restricted. They are, of course, free to reject the stereotyped expectations of themselves as potential wives but greater personal consequences are attendant upon such a course. As Mr. Collins reminds Elizabeth, "It is by no means certain that another offer of marriage may ever be made you. Your portion is unhappily so small that it will in all likelihood undo the effects of your loveliness and amiable qualifacations." (*P & P*, 82) Contrary to Mr. Collins' dire prediction, however, Elizabeth does not suffer the fate of the penniless redundant woman. On the most basic level, of course, she is spared this fate through her happy marriage to Mr. Darcy. But Elizabeth's happy ending is the result, and not the cause, of her integration into her society. Her marriage is an outward sign of an interior victory: the fact that she has employed her intelligence and sensitivity to attain a self-definition which is at once true to her own best self and acceptable to her society. Not all of the heroines attain the poise which Elizabeth eventually achieves: Jane Eyre finds her happiness in a union which excludes society; Dorothea's marriage to Will is fully satisfactory neither to herself nor to her society; Maggie Tulliver dies an outcast from her social world. However different the results of their struggles, the process of the heroines' strivings towards self-definition is a distinctly engaging one: for they are involved in the same basic conflict between being and functioning, between the forces of depersonalization and the need for self-assertion which confronts women and men today.

ELIZABETH BENNET

Elizabeth Bennet is a heroine whom Mrs. Sarah Ellis would probably disown as a "daughter of England." Elizabeth refuses to define herself according to her mother's materialistic values or to adopt her father's socially irresponsible attitude. Mrs. Bennet's character is acidly delineated very early in *Pride and Prejudice*:

> *She was a woman of mean understanding, little information, and uncertain temper. When she was discontented she fancied herself nervous. The business of her life was to get her daughters married; its solace was visiting and news.* (P & P, 3)

Elizabeth's intellectual acuity and wit stand in direct contrast to her mother's "mean understanding" and "little information." Mrs. Bennet's cold-blooded view of marriage as a "business" conflicts with Elizabeth's moral sensitivity and with her personal aspiration to marry only upon the basis of love and mutual esteem. The wisdom of Elizabeth's rejection of her mother's standards is clearly illustrated through the fate of her sister Lydia. Lydia is Mrs. Bennet's favorite daughter because, in her vulgarity and sensuality, Lydia represents a personification of Mrs. Bennet as a young girl. Mrs. Bennet identifies with Lydia to the extent of defending her daughter's reckless flirting with the soldiers of the Meryton regiment: "I remember the time when I liked a red coat myself very well--and indeed so I do still at my heart." (P & P, 21) Lydia proceeds to complete the identification between herself and her mother by entering a marriage based, like her mother's and father's, on superficial sexual attraction.

Since Mrs. Bennet embodies the basest and most vulgar aspects of her materialistic society, Elizabeth is clearly unable to define herself as her mother's daughter. Neither, however, can she accept the flippant, a-social irresponsibility which characterizes her father's attitude towards society. Mr. Bennet's witty remark—"For what do we live, but to make sport for our neighbours, and laugh at them in our turn? " (*P & P*, 272)--is amusing on a superficial level. But it reveals an improper, excessive detachment of himself from even the legitimate involvement with society which his duty as a father demands. His extreme indifference forces Elizabeth to effect a role reversal. Instead of being able to rely on his fatherly guidance and counsel, Elizabeth must assume the dominant role of advising Mr. Bennet of his parental duties and responsibilities.

Unable to follow the example of her mother's total acceptance of social values or of her father's complete dismissal of them, Elizabeth must work out her own self-definition with only her intelligence and sensitivity to guide her. Her basic stance is an a-typical and unconventional one. Viewing herself as an inherently valuable and unique person, Elizabeth rejects her society's stereotyped expectations and its depersonalizing assessment of herself as an available commodity on the block of a social marriage market.,

Elizabeth's unconventionality can best be measured against the functions which her society expects a marriageable young woman to perform. Miss Bingley summarizes these expectations:

> *"No one can be really esteemed accomplished, who does not greatly surpass what is usually met with. A woman must have a thorough knowledge of music, singing, drawing, dancing and the modern languages, to deserve the word; and besides all this, she must possess a certain something in her air and manner of walking, the tone of her voice, her address and expressions, or the word will be but half deserved."*
> (P & P, *29*)

Elizabeth, according to the Bingley sisters, certainly lacks that "certain something in her air and manner of walking." After an energetic three-mile walk, Elizabeth's appearance is judged to be most unconventionally "wild."[11] The Bingley sisters are quick to criticize Elizabeth's "untidy, blowsy" hair, her petticoat "six inches deep in mud," her "conceited independence" and "indifference to decorum." (P & P, 26) Elizabeth also fails to exhibit the stereotyped musical accomplishments. She later explains to Darcy:

> "My fingers . . . do not move over this instrument in the masterly manner which I see so many women's do. They have not the same force or rapidity, and do not produce the same expression. But then I have always supposed it to be my own fault--because I would not take the trouble of practising. It is not that I do not believe my fingers as capable as any other woman's of superior execution." (P & P, 132)

The real offence which Elizabeth renders the Bingley sisters and, by extension, all of society, is not her unconventional appearance nor her lack of musical accomplishment. Rather, she offends their sensibilities because she refuses to value such stereotyped accomplishments or to lament her own lack of them. Because of her intelligence and independence, Elizabeth is able to amuse herself according to her own tastes. The Bingleys find her preference for reading over card playing to be threatening. Since she herself is limited by her stereotyped definition of herself as a potential wife, Caroline Bingley can judge Elizabeth's singular preference for reading only in terms of competition.

> "Eliza Bennet," said Miss Bingley . . . "is one of those young ladies who seek to recommend themselves to the other sex, by undervaluing their own; and with many men, I dare say, it succeeds. But, in my opinion, it is a paltry device, a mean art." (P & P, 29)

So preoccupied is Miss Bingley with winning the race to the altar, that she fails to realize that Elizabeth has not even entered the competition.

When Mr. Collins proposes marriage, Elizabeth is forced to defend herself against the stereotyped expectations of her society. Mr. Collins cannot see Elizabeth as a person but only as a stereotyped object: she is a girl without a fortune who must therefore desire to marry. Elizabeth's initially sincere and polite refusal is, to Mr. Collins, merely part of the role which all young woman play:

71

"I am not now to learn . . . that it is usual with young ladies to reject the addresses of the man whom they secretly mean to accept, when he first applies for their favour; and that sometimes the refusal is repeated a second or even a third time. I am therefore by no means discouraged by what you have just said, and shall hope to lead you to the altar ere long." (P & P, 81)

Elizabeth's repeated and increasingly heated attempts to force Mr. Collins to see her as a real human being with personal aspirations to happiness meet with no success. She entreats Mr. Collins to view her as she sees herself: "a rational creature speaking the truth from her heart." (*P & P*, 83) But her efforts are futile; Mr. Collins persists in his conception of Elizabeth as an "elegant female" attempting, "according to the usual practice," to increase his love by suspense. (*P & P*, 82)

Mr. Collins' obdurate blindness illustrates how culturally established sex roles can be mutually depersonalizing. While Elizabeth is insulted at his refusal to acknowledge her independent existence, aspirations and desires, Mr. Collins appears almost dehumanized as he mechanically observes the rituals which he considers to be a regular part of the "business" of proposing marriage.

Just as Elizabeth refuses to accept Mr. Collins' assessment of herself as a marriagable commodity, she also rejects Lady Catherine De Bourgh's attempt to define her worth according to her material wealth and social standing. Lady Catherine sees Elizabeth as an unpleasant object: a young woman of upstart pretensions without family, connections, or fortune. Although Elizabeth has, at this time, no assurance of regaining Darcy's love, she refuses to allow Lady Catherine to treat her as a mere irritant to her match-making plans. Elizabeth asserts her own independence and refuses to be cowed by wealth and status when she declines to promise Lady Catherine that she will never enter into an engagement with Mr. Darcy.

Elizabeth's struggle for self-definition is certainly complicated by the limitations which accrue to the condition of being female. Her struggle is rendered even more painful by virtue of the extreme sensitivity which she, as a talented heroine, possesses. At the same time, Elizabeth's problem is part of the larger dilemma of the human need to be true to oneself. Elizabeth's unconventional refusal to define herself as daughter or as a potential wife stems from her innate sense of worth as a person, quite apart from economic or social considerations. Under the influence of her growing love for Darcy, Elizabeth's self-esteem is strengthened as she progressively comes to realize how she and Darcy might complement and complete each other's personalities. When she visits Pemberley, Darcy's estate, the rhetoric of her response to its beauty is significant. Elizabeth felt, Jane Austen tells us, "that to be mistress of Pemberley might be something." (*P & P*, 181) The repetition of the verb "to be" illustrates Elizabeth's unique awareness of the distinction between "being" and "doing" or between being and function. She realizes that self-fulfillment and social roles are not inherently contradictory. Through a union of love and mutual respect Elizabeth will simultaneously perform a social function--as mistress of Pemberley--and yet "be something"--a person in her own right.

Elizabeth does achieve this poise at the end of *Pride and Prejudice*, and this should not surprise us. Despite her unconventionality, Elizabeth has demonstrated a respect for the opinion of society where matters of real moral substance were concerned. Her sense of justice was outraged when she felt that Darcy had exposed her sister Jane to society's "derision for disappointed hopes" (*P & P*, 144); her moral sensitivity compelled her to attempt to restrain Lydia's immorality which threatened to ruin the reputation of her family. Elizabeth's self-image, we recall, was not of herself as a rebel but as a perceiver. She possesses the discriminating ability to reject what is false and hollow in society while retaining those expectations which she perceives to be based upon valid moral principles.

EMMA WOODHOUSE

While Elizabeth Bennet finds it impossible to define herself in terms of the socially approved role of daughter another Austen heroine, Emma Woodhouse, readily embraces the role which Elizabeth rejects. Mr. Woodhouse is a kindly, ineffectual egoist and Emma's relationship to her father reveals much about her unconventional aspirations and her self-image. Emma chooses to define herself according to the expectations of her society: she is a gentleman's daughter. Mrs. Weston, Emma's former governess, summarizes the way in which Emma appears to the members of her society:

> "*With all dear Emma's little faults, she is an excellent crea-
> ture. Where shall we see a better daughter, or a kinder*

sister, or a truer friend?" (E, 25)

These functions of daughter, sister and friend seem to be strangely limited choices for an aspiring and intelligent heroine. Emma chooses to adopt these stereotyped roles because they offer her the freedom to fulfill her unconscious image of herself as a benign manipulator and they afford a respectable social front for her aspirations to power.

Mr. Woodhouse's confused mind, his hypochondria, and his childish self-absorption render him totally powerless as a father. As in the case of Elizabeth and Mr. Bennet, the parent-child roles are reversed in the relationship of Emma and Mr. Woodhouse. Emma directs, consoles, and, most importantly, manipulates her father precisely as a mother controls her dependent child. When, during the party at the Weston's, snow begins to fall, Mr. Woodhouse exhibits his typically exaggerated, confused, and helpless response:

> *"What is to be done, my dear Emma?--what is to be done?"*
> *was Mr. Woodhouse's first exclamation, and all that he could*
> *say for some time. To her he looked for comfort; and her*
> *assurances of safety, her representation of the excellence of*
> *the horses, and of James, and of their having so many friends*
> *about them, revived him a little. (E, 86)*

While it is true that Mr. Woodhouse sometimes exploits his own weaknesses in order to control Emma, it is also true that Emma uses her father in far more subtle ways. On the most basic level, he presents an object upon which she can exercise her manipulative powers. His helplessness places Emma in a position of complete power at Hartfield. While Emma genuinely tries to please her father by arranging social gatherings for him, her real satisfaction derives from the opportunity to dominate which these affairs afford:

> *These were the ladies [Mrs. and Miss Bates, Mrs. Goodard]*
> *whom Emma found herself very frequently able to* collect;
> *and happy was she, for her father's sake, in the* power; . . .
> *She was delighted to see her father look comfortable, and*
> *very much pleased with herself for* contriving *things so well.*
> *(E, 13. Emphasis added)*

This passage reveals how Emma exploits her social role as Mr. Woodhouse's daughter in order to reinforce her unconscious self-image. Emma views the

74

three ladies as depersonalized objects which she can "collect," she rejoices in her "power" of social manipulation and, significantly, she is pleased with her own ability to contrive and to dominate. It is remarkable how often Emma manages to disguise her need to dominate through playing the role of the dutiful daughter. When Mr. Woodhouse's neurotic dining habits deprive Mrs. Bates and Mrs. Goodard of a substantial dinner, Emma offers them cake and wine in an effort to "make the two ladies all the amends in her *power* . . . for what ever unwilling self-denial his [Mr. Woodhouse's] care of their constitution might have obliged them to practise during the meal." (*E*, 143. Emphasis added) Even the size of the dining table provides Emma with a reflection of her power: ". . . Mr. Knightley must take his seat with the rest around the large circular table which Emma had introduced at Hartfield, and which none but Emma could have had the power to place there and persuade her father to use. (*E*, 236-237)

Emma really only appears to define herself in terms of her role as daughter. She merely exploits this and other social roles in order to attain a greater degree of individual freedom. She cleverly uses her function as daughter as a defense against another stereotyped function: society's definition of her as a potential wife. Emma's view of marriage appears to be most unconventional. She defends Harriet Smith's refusal of Robert Martin against Mr. Knightley's criticism:

> *"Oh! to be sure," cried Emma, "it is always incomprehensible to a man that a woman should ever refuse an offer of marriage. A man always imagines a woman to be ready for anybody who asks her."* (E, 40)

Her heated criticism of the conventional qualities which men expect in a potential wife would not be unworthy of the most ardent feminist:

> *"She [Harriet Smith] is not a clever girl, but she has better sense than you are aware of, and does not deserve to have her understanding spoken of so slightingly. Waving that point, however, and supposing her to be . . . only pretty and good-natured, let me tell you . . . they are not trivial recommendations to the world in general . . . and till it appears that men are much more philosophic on the subject of beauty than they are generally supposed; till they do fall in love with well-informed minds instead of handsome faces, a girl, with*

such lovliness as Harriet, has a certainty of being admired and
sought after . . ." (E, 42)

It would be tempting, on the basis of this passage alone, to judge Emma to be the most unconventional of all the heroines on the question of marriage. Even Elizabeth Bennet, in her speech to Mr. Collins, does not go so far as to condemn the entire system of courtship or to criticize the stereotyped expectations of men in general. Elizabeth and Jane Eyre, two of the most outspoken heroines, both tend to restrict their criticisms of marriage to their own immediate personal situations. Elizabeth urgently wants Mr. Collins to see her as a real person and not as a mere commodity, but she does not openly condemn the system which has encouraged his limited vision. Similarly, Jane Eyre refuses Rochester and St. John Rivers for personal reasons: because the particular unions which they offer would violate her selfhood. Jane does not, however, condemn Rochester's sexual desires or St. John's pragmatic ones as typical examples of the superficiality of men's marital expectations.

Emma does, indeed, go further than any of the heroines in her attack upon the artificiality of socially established sex roles. She seems to be defending Harriet's mind as well as exposing a real flaw in the social structure of her world. Men in the nineteenth century, in fact and fiction, did overwhelmingly prefer "handsome faces" to "well-informed minds". Lydgate's choice of Rosamund, Stephen's infatuation with Lucy Deane, Rochester's marriage to Bertha Mason are but a few illustrations of this propensity. Socially ambitious young women were aware of this fact and countless numbers of them heeded Dr. Gregory's advice by hiding their wit, concealing their good sense and keeping their learning a "profound secret."[12]

Emma's response to Mr. Knightley, however assertive it may appear, is truly unconventional only in the sense that Emma defies Dr. Gregory's legacy by displaying her wit before a marriageable gentleman. Emma's real concern, in her exchange with Knightley, is to justify her own manipulative treatment of Harriet Smith. In appearing to defend Harriet, Emma is really defending herself for she views Harriet, her protege and her creation, as an extension of herself. Emma speaks the truth when she describes the stereotyped marital expectations which men hold, but she is not in any way committed to rectifying the unjust results of these expectations. Her insensitive treatment of Miss Bates and Jane Fairfax, two unmarried women in her society, illustrates the superficiality of her concern for women's condition. Moreover, Emma is not theoretically opposed to marriage where other people are concerned. She constantly conspires, actively and imaginatively, to effect marital matches which will reflect favorably upon her manipulative powers.

Emma objects to marriage only where she herself is concerned. She exploits her role as daughter in order to provide a socially acceptable reason for her unconventional stance. When Emma fancies herself to be in love with Frank Churchill, her imaginary romance stops short of marriage:

> *The conclusion of every imaginary declaration on his [Frank's] side was that she [Emma] refused him. Their affection was always to subside into friendship. Every thing tender and charming was to mark their parting; but still they were to part. When she became sensible of this, it struck her that she could not be very much in love; for in spite of her previous and fixed determination never to quit her father, never to marry, a strong attachment certainly must produce more of a struggle than she could foresee in her own feelings.*
> *(E, 179)*

Emma's decision "never to quit her father" is, in part, motivated by sincere affection and solicitude. But Emma also rejects the idea of marriage because she is unconsciously unwilling to surrender either her power or her detachment. Emma realizes that her position as mistress of Hartfield affords her a degree of social power and independence which she will be denied in even the best marriage:

> *"I believe few married women are half as much mistress of their husband's house, as I am of Hartfield; and never, never could I expect to be so truly beloved and important; so always first and always right in any man's eyes as I am in my father's." (E, 58)*

Emma is, however, unaware of the fear of commitment which her speech reveals. Marriage in the Austen world demands the kind of total involvement of self with society which would automatically thwart Emma's aspirations to power. In order to dominate effectively, Emma must retain her detached s stance vis a vis her society. She needs to be in her society but not of it: to be able to work behind the scenes, pulling the proper strings to manipulate the puppet-people of her world. In resisting marriage and the functions of wife-hood, Emma is fighting to retain her unconscious image of herself as the powerful benign manipulator.

When Emma unwittingly finds herself involved in her society at the Box Hill outing, her efforts to regain her sense of detachment lead her into a display of real moral insensitivity. Emma becomes uncomfortable and irritable upon this occasion for two main reasons. Primarily, she is uneasy because she is not in command of the situation. It is not her party, but Mr. Weston's and the affair is not organized to Emma's liking:

> There was a languor, a want of spirits, a want of union, which could not be got over. They separated too much into parties. The Eltons walked together; Mr. Knightley took charge of Miss Bates and Jane; and Emma and Harriet belonged to Frank Churchill. (E, 251)

The diffuse nature of this social situation threatens Emma by limiting her access to the knowledge and the sense of omniscience which has allowed her to dominate other social affairs. If people will persist in isolating themselves into various social cliques, one must make a choice to join one group or another. Since Emma cannot be everywhere--she is "assigned" to Frank Churchill --she is denied the kind of knowledge about other people's feelings, thoughts, and reactions which her acute perception usually affords her in social situations.

More particularly, Emma is uneasy because of the behavior of Frank Churchill. Frank fails to fulfill the function which Emma had mentally assigned to him: instead of acting as her friend, Frank performs the role of lover in an outrageously flirtatious manner. Emma does realize, however, that Frank is in command of the situation and that he is exploiting her in order to gain the attention of the entire party.

Emma finds herself involved in an intricate and potentially explosive social situation which is seemingly beyond her control. The only available defense which Emma can employ is detachment. In order to regain her singularity, to isolate herself from a situation which threatens her, Emma displays her wit at the expense of Miss Bates. Her unkind, cutting remark to Miss Bates has the desired effect. The tension of the social situation is broken and the attention of the party is diverted from Frank Churchill and herself.

Essentially, Emma has used Miss Bates as a comic object to relieve her own sense of discomfort and social unease. When Mr. Knightley upbraids Emma for her conduct, he points to her essential failure to fulfill the social role of "friend" to Miss Bates. Because of her character, age, and indigent unmarried state, Miss Bates has social claims to the kindness and respect of the wealthy, clever, accomplished Miss Woodhouse. Jane Fairfax, too, because she is a respectable young woman without a fortune is entitled, by society's standards, to Emma's friendship and solicitude. Emma recognizes the social code of the "duty of woman by woman" (*E*, 156) but she is unable sincerely to perform the role of "friend" either to Miss Bates or Jane Fairfax. Miss Bates annoys Emma because she is neither intelligent nor interesting: Miss Bates has "no intellecutal superiority to make atonement to herself, or frighten those who might hate her, into outward respect." (*E*, 12) Jane Fairfax, as we have seen, alienates Emma because Jane's reserve frustrates Emma's desire for dominance. Until Emma sheds her illusory self-image, she is capable of acting as a "friend" only to people who, like Harriet Smith, are interesting, malleable, and easily manipulated.

It is significant that Emma takes refuge from her uncomfortable experience of involvement with her society at Box Hill in her home and her daughterly duties. Stung by Mr. Knightley's severe reproaches, Emma consoles herself for her failure to perform the role of friend by meditating upon her successful performance of her functions as daughter:

> *The wretchedness of a scheme to Box Hill was in Emma's thoughts all the evening . . . in her view it was a morning more completely misspent, more totally bare of rational satisfaction at the time, and more to be abhorred in recollection, than any she had ever passed. A whole evening of back-gammon with her father, was felicity to it. There indeed, lay real pleasure, for there she was giving up the sweetest hours of the twenty-four to his comfort; and feeling that, unmerited as might be the degree of his fond affection and confiding esteem, she could not, in her general conduct, be open to any severe reproach. As a daughter, she hoped she was not without a heart. (E, 258)*

Emma is not really "without a heart." Although she unconsciously manipulates her father, she endures his eccentric demands with endless patience.

She is truly generous to the poor in her parish and she is unfailingly sensitive to the needs of her sister Isabella.

Just as Emma's genuine love for her father enables her to fulfill his demands with graciousness and respect, her love for Isabella affords her with another socially acceptable role: that of the devoted sister and loving aunt. Emma is genuinely devoted to her nephew and niece and even the critical Mr. Knightley observes the naturalness of her affection for them. Emma imagines that she is expressing the appropriate concern of an aunt when she objects to Mrs. Weston's "match" between Mr. Knightley and Jane Fairfax:

> *"Mr. Knightley and Jane Fairfax! . . . Dear Mrs. Weston, how could you think of such a thing? --Mr. Knightley must not marry!--You would not have little Henry cut out from Donwell? --Oh! no, no, Henry must have Donwell." (E, 151)*

Only later does Emma realize how she has used her social function as the concerned aunt to suppress her own unconscious love for Mr. Knightley and her jealousy at the very thought of his marrying anyone but herself.

Emma's attempt to define her unique, unconventional and aspiring character in terms of such stereotyped social roles as those of daughter, friend, and aunt ultimately fails because this self-definition is a basically insincere attempt to reinforce her illusory self-image. Although Emma's choice to define herself solely in terms of social roles was a conscious one, "functionalism" has nevertheless had a depersonalizing effect upon her character. Her conscious limitations of her spontaneity, in order to conform to social expectations, were really a form of self-deception and hypocrisy. Emma sought to deceive the world by assuming outwardly acceptable social roles which would free her to exercise her essentially anti-social manipulative desires. Her compulsive need to retain her sense of detachment led Emma to view other persons, such as Miss Bates and Jane Fairfax, in a dehumanized way. When Emma realizes the illusory nature of her self-image and becomes conscious of her love for Mr. Knightley she no longer requires the defenses of her former self-definitions, for she no longer desires to manipulate from afar. By falling in love with Mr. Knightley, Emma had unconsciously committed herself. Her conscious decision to marry him indicates her mature willingness to involve herself in her society in a fully human way.

MAGGIE TULLIVER

Maggie Tulliver, like Emma Woodhouse, defines herself in terms of the social and familial roles of daughter and sister. The chief difference between these two heroines' self-definitions is that Emma consciously assumes a social role which is at odds with her interior self-image while Maggie unconsciously, without any ulterior motive, accepts and strives to fulfill society's expectations for herself. Maggie's image of herself as child harmonizes perfectly with her self-definition; Emma's self-image, by way of contrast, constantly conflicts with her outwardly assumed roles of daughter, sister, aunt and friend. Maggie's defining herself in terms of social functions has a far more destructive impact upon her personality than does Emma's. Emma is eventually educated out of the limitations of her self-definition; Maggie dies a prisoner of her own inadequate self-image and self-definition.

The destructive effects of Maggie's definition of herself as Tom's sister and Mr. Tulliver's daughter begin in Maggie's childhood. Maggie is particularly drawn to her father because of his warmth and spontaneity; Mr. Tulliver sees in Maggie a reflection of himself:

> "It seems a bit of a pity, though," said Mr. Tulliver, "as the lad should take after the mother's side instead o' the little wench. That's the worst on't w' the crossing o' breeds: you can never justly calkilate what'll come on't. The little un takes after my side, now: she's twice as 'cute as Tom. Too 'cute for a woman, I'm afraid." (MF, 12)

Although Mr. Tulliver identifies with Maggie and recognizes her intellectual superiority to her brother, he fulfills society's expectations by sending Tom to school and ruefully regretting how Maggie's intelligence will lessen her value as a marriageable commodity.

Her father's denigration of her intelligence has its effect upon the sensitive Maggie. She assumes Tom's practical knowledge of such natural phenomena as worms, fish, birds, etc. to be infinitely superior to her own:

> Maggie thought this sort of knowledge was very wonderful--
> much more difficult than remembering what was in books;
> and she was rather in awe of Tom's superiority, for he was

> *the only person who called her knowledge "stuff," and did*
> *not feel surprised at her cleverness. (MF, 36)*

Maggie's sense of inferiority to Tom extends even to their fishing expeditions. She thinks it probable that "the small fish would come to her hook, and the large ones to Tom's." (*MF*, 36) She is pleasantly surprised when she manages to catch a large fish and to please Tom at the same time. Maggie's achievement pleases her because she has, remarkably, been able to excel at something which Tom values. She defines herself in terms of Tom's values and her childhood ambition is to prolong this self-definition into adulthood. She tells Luke, the head miller: "I love Tom so dearly, Luke--better than anybody else in the world. When he grows up I shall keep his house, and we shall always live together." (*MF*, 28) This little speech of Maggie's is poignant in its irony. Her love for Tom will later compel her to perform an act of renunciation which will cause Tom to bar her from the very home she had hoped to share with him.

Maggie's love for Tom leads her to attempt to identify herself with him. When she visits Tom at Mr. Stelling's school, she tries to imitate him by studying the Latin Grammar which Tom finds so frustrating and puzzling. Maggie's intellectual prowess and imaginative sense cause her to find the Grammar both delightful and fascinating. Tom's shaky ego is threatened by Maggie's intellectual quickness. When Maggie declares that she is sure she could learn geometry, Tom turns to the voice of authority, Mr. Stelling, in order to remind Maggie of her feminine inferiority:

> *"Mr. Stelling," she [Maggie] said, . . . "couldn't I do Euclid, and all Tom's lessons, if you were to teach me instead of him?"*
> *"No; you couldn't," said Tom, indignantly. "Girls can't do Euclid: can they, sir?"*
> *"They can pick up a little of everything, I daresay," said Mr. Stelling. "They've a great deal of superficial cleverness; but they couldn't go far into anything. They're quick and shallow." (MF, 133-134)*

Mr. Stelling speaks for Maggie's society in his conventional assessment of the female intellect as essentially shallow and superficial. Maggie, like Dorothea Brooke, is destined to receive a "toy-box history of the world adapted to young ladies" (*MF*, 63) instead of a real education.

Maggie's visit to Mr. Stelling's school reveals her innate intellectual superiority to Tom and the degree to which her intellectual aspirations conflict with her self-definition. When Maggie asserts her intention of being a "clever woman," the ensuing dialogue between her and Tom is prophetic:

> "But I shall be a clever woman," said Maggie, with a toss.
> "Oh, I daresay, and a nasty conceited thing. Everybody 'll hate you."
> "But you oughtn't to hate me, Tom: it'll be very wicked of you, for I shall be your sister."
> "Yes, but if you're a nasty, disagreeable thing, I shall hate you." (MF, 130)

Tom, despite his youth, is already thoroughly imbued with the conventional view of women which his society holds. Essentially, he is warning Maggie that she cannot have it both ways: she cannot assume the conventional definition of herself as Tom's sister if she defies society's standards by becoming a "clever woman." Tom correctly predicts that Maggie's unconventionality will ultimately cause him to reject her. Maggie remains impervious to his warning because of her emotional and unreflecting nature. She can only understand the claims of love: because she is Tom's sister, it follows naturally to Maggie that Tom should always love her. Tom's notion that principles and propriety may supercede the claims of love and fidelity is alien and incomprehensible to Maggie.

Maggie's definition of herself as Tom's sister is in direct conflict with her definition of herself as Mr. Tulliver's daughter. In his practicality, lack of imagination, and devotion to material values, Tom is a true Dodson. In her impetuosity, emotionalism and loving, unreflecting nature, Maggie is truly her father's daughter. The inherent conflict in Maggie's self-definition remains subtle and largely dormant during Maggie's childhood. After Mr. Tulliver's financial disaster, however, the opposing forces of Dodson and Tulliver are clearly revealed. Although her husband is severely ill, Mrs. Tulliver's only thoughts are for the loss of material goods and social prestige which Mr. Tulliver's impractical impetuosity has brought about. Mrs. Tulliver is a pathetic example of the moral bankruptcy of the Dodson values as she weeps over her china, silver and linen while reproaching her husband: "And to think as he should ha' married me, and brought me to this." (MF, 180) Tom shares his mother's materialistic values and he inwardly turns against his father. At this point, Maggie can no longer identify with Tom; her moral sensitivity, sense of justice, and emotional affinity to her father cause her to take his part:

> Maggie had witnessed this scene with gathering anger. The implied reproaches against her father--her father, who was lying there in a sort of living death--neutralised all her pity for griefs about table-cloths and china; and her anger on her father's account was heightened by some egoistic resentment at Tom's silent concurrence with her mother in shutting her out from the common calamity . . . she burst out at last in an agitated, almost violent tone, "Mother, how can you talk so? as if you cared only for things with your name on, and not for what has my father's name too--and to care about anything but dear father himself!--when he's lying there, and may never speak to us again. Tom, you ought to say so too-- you ought not to let anyone find fault with my father."
> (MF, 181)

It is a sign of Maggie's complete identification with Mr. Tulliver that she constantly uses the singular possessive adjective: he is *her* father, "my father." The fact that she recognizes she can no longer define herself in terms of both Tom and her father is indicated by her failure to consider Mr. Tulliver as Tom's father also; not once does she employ the phrase "our father" in speaking to Tom about Mr. Tulliver.

It would seem that her family's misfortune offers Maggie an opportunity to escape the limitations of her former self-definition as Tom's sister. She recognizes that her values and Tom's are inexorably opposed and she has attained an insight into the superiority of her moral sensitivity to Tom's harsh practicality. In siding with her father, she seems to have consciously chosen the kind of loving, humanistic standards which will enable her personality to flower and attain self-fulfillment.

This open schism between the Dodson and the Tulliver standards is, unfortunately for Maggie, of short duration. Although Mr. Tulliver recovers from his stroke, he never again regains his position as head of the household. Mr. Tulliver delegates this authority to Tom in a ritualistic ceremony of vengeance. When Tom signs his name to Mr. Tulliver's curse upon Lawyer Wakem, the values of father and son are merged: they are united in a solemn pledge to seek retribution, revenge, and the downfall of their mutual enemy, Maggie can no longer assert her loyalty to "her" father's values as opposed to Tom's. If she wishes to continue to define herself in terms of familial relationships, the only way of self-definition which she knows, she must once more fulfill the now complementary roles of daughter and sister.

During the lonely period of depressing poverty, isolation and deprivation which follows Mr. Tulliver's bankruptcy, Maggie feels alienated both from Tom and her father. Tom is obsessed with his driving ambition to carry out his father's desire to regain the ownership of the mill and Mr. Tulliver himself has regressed into a depressive, childlike state of dependency and petulance. Maggie makes several attempts to achieve a new self-definition through asceticism, work and her friendship with Philip. Her attempt at renunciation fails because, as we have seen, it is an essentially immature and superficial kind of asceticism which Maggie embraces. Her effort to find sewing work and her relationship with Philip are healthy and potentially liberating attempts at a larger sense of self; both of these efforts are, however, frustrated by Tom. Maggie's determination to take in plain sewing in order to relieve her family's financial situation indicates a sensitive and unselfish desire actively to contribute to her family's improvement. Tom, however, interprets her efforts as a threat to his authority and masculinity. Moreover, Maggie's unconventionality disturbs Tom. Society decrees that respectable women, even if their families are on the brink of starvation, simply do not enter linen shops and ask for work: "I don't like *my* sister to do such things," said Tom; "*I'll* take care that the debts are paid, without your lowering yourself in that way." (*MF*, 256-257)

Maggie further offends Tom's conventional sensibilities because she violates what John Langdon-Davies has called the myth of "The Female Character." The sole object of a woman's character, according to this myth was ". . . to please men and to avoid anything which might 'harden' the woman, any work intellectual or manual which might weight down with mundane contacts the ethereal nothingness of her complacent character. This is in short parisitism."[13]

Maggie's friendship with Philip Wakem, while it threatens her image of herself as a child, offers her liberation from her functionalised self-definition. Philip affords Maggie the opportunity and encouragement to develop a sense of herself as a unique person with individual tastes, aspirations and opinions. Tom cleverly exploits Maggie's devotion to her father in order to end her friendship with Philip. Maggie agrees to tell the particulars of their relationship only "for my father's sake." (*MF*, 321) Tom then presents Maggie with a choice which opposes her life-long definition of herself as a dutiful daughter to her budding spirit of independence:

> "*Now, then, Maggie, there are but two courses for you to take; either you vow solemnly to me, with your hand on my father's Bible, that you will never have another meeting or speak another word in private with Philip Wakem, or you refuse, and I tell my father everything; and this month, when by my exertions he might be made happy once more, you will cause him the blow of knowing that you are a disobedient, deceitful daughter, who throws away her own respectability by clandestine meetings with the son of a man that has helped to ruin her father. Choose!*" (MF, 300)

Tom's choice, of course, really offers Maggie no options at all. He simply offers her variant ways of realizing her role as daughter: she can be a good, dutiful daughter or a "disobedient, deceitful" one. The real issue, which Tom's vision is too limited and Maggie's too clouded by emotion to see, is whether Maggie shall continue to define herself--either positively or negatively--according to the restricted functions of her role as daughter or whether she will reach out for the freedom and potential self-fulfillment to which Philip has exposed her. In view of Maggie's character, her decision is a foregone conclusion. Her love for Tom and her father, her self-image and her need for a sense of self-definition unite to compel her assent to Tom's wishes.

Unlike Elizabeth Bennet and Emma Woodhouse, Maggie has not had to erect defenses against society's definition of a young woman as a potential wife. Because of her family's financial situation, Maggie has been isolated from the larger society of St. Ogg's and she is, by society's standards, a decidedly poor marriage prospect. Mr. Tulliver, who is ever alert to the opinions of society, meditates bitterly that Maggie "had a poor chance for marrying, down in the world as they were." (*MF*, 245) When Maggie makes her debut into St. Ogg society, under the patronage of her cousin Lucy, the most striking aspect of her social behavior is her unconventionality. Maggie's social unconventionality is not, as Elizabeth Bennet's is, a calculated stance or a determined assertion of her individuality. Rather, her social conduct, like Jane Eyre's, illustrates her complete lack of familiarity with the stereotyped conventions of her larger social world. Maggie has additional affinities with Jane Eyre, and with Jane Fairfax of *Emma*, in that she, like them, bears the social stigma of having to "take a situation"--a delicate euphemism for the social disgrace of having to earn one's own living by teaching.

Maggie's former society has consisted of the extremely limited circle of her family and Philip. Within this familial society, she struggled to fulfill certain functionalised roles. When she enters the society of St. Ogg's after her father's death, Maggie has the illusion of freedom. She does not realize that this larger social world is every bit as functionalised in its view of women as was her more limited environment. Lawyer Wakem epitomizes the opinion of St. Ogg society: "We don't ask what a woman does--we ask whom she belongs to." (*MF*, 372) Maggie "belongs to" the Tulliver family in a dual sense: her society automatically defines her as the daughter of a man who died in disgrace and this definition reinforces Maggie's own sense that her selfhood is dependent upon past ties and fidelities.

Maggie's social unconventionality is most dramatically illustrated in her inability to play out the stereotyped niceties which constitute the basis of male-female relationships. She is unable to be coy, ornamental, or charmingly frivolous. When Stephen Guest pays the traditional gentlemanly compliment to her beauty, Maggie recoils from the artificiality of the social situation: "Now you have proved yourself equal to the occasion . . . and said what it was incumbent on you to say under the circumstances." (*MF*, 328) What appears to be gratuitous rudeness on Maggie's part is merely a manifestation of her naturalness and innate sincerity:

> *She was so unused to society that she could take nothing as a matter of course, and had never in her life spoken from the lips merely, so that she must necessarily appear absurd to more experienced ladies . . . (MF, 329)*

Maggie further offends the social proprieties by freely admitting that her skill in plain sewing does not represent an accomplishment but a means of earning her living. This confession brings a blush to the cheek of the conventional little Lucy. Paradoxically, however, this extraordinary lack of social finesse increases Maggie's appeal to men. Eliot notes that "if Maggie had been the queen of coquettes she could hardly have invented a means of giving greater piquancy to her beauty in Stephen's eyes." (*MF*, 330) Philip Wakem, too, is attracted by Maggie's lack of pretension. He tells his father: "She's very tender and affectionate; and so simple--without the airs and petty contrivances other women have." (*MF*, 375)

The attraction which Maggie holds for Stephen and Philip is a commentary on the mutually depersonalizing effects which stereotyped social roles impose. Maggie intrigues both men because she responds to them as persons and, however indecorous her responses, they are always sincere. Maggie does not conduct herself with the polished artificiality of the husband-hungry young lady. However engaging Philip and Stephen find her spontaneity, the society of St. Ogg's disapproves of her in much the same way that the Bingley sisters criticized Elizabeth:

> *The Miss Guests, who associated chiefly on terms of condescension with the families of St. Ogg's, and were the glass of fashion there, took some exception to Maggie's manners. She had a way of not assenting at once to the observations current in good society, and of saying that she didn't know whether those observations were true or not, which gave her an air of gaucherie, and impeded the even flow of conversation. . . . And Maggie was so entirely without those pretty airs of coquetry which have the traditional reputation of driving gentlemen to despair, that she won some feminine pity for being so ineffective in spite of her beauty. She had not many advantages, poor thing!* (MF, 349)

It is ironic that the lack of coquetry which, in society's opinion, renders Maggie unattractive to gentlemen is the very quality which Stephen Guest finds so engaging. The "feminine pity" which society so effortlessly lavishes on Maggie turns quickly to ostracism when Maggie returns, unmarried, after her aborted elopement with Stephen. Society cannot forgive Maggie for her failure to define herself as Mrs. Stephen Guest. The "world's wife" does not disapprove of Maggie on moral or ethical grounds; indeed, if she had fulfilled conventional expectations, she would have been welcomed as a most romantically exciting addition to her society:

> *If Miss Tulliver, after a few months of well-chosen travel, had returned as Mrs. Stehpen Guest--with a post-marital*

trousseau, *and all the advantages possessed even by the most unwelcome wife of an only son, public opinion . . . would have judged in strict consistency with these results.* (MF, 428)

Essentially, Maggie is condemned because she has failed to live out the stereotyped progression of social roles. In eloping with Stephen she indicated to society that she was exchanging the role of daughter and sister for the functions of wifehood. When Maggie realizes that her marriage to Stephen would violate her definition of herself as a dutiful daughter, obedient sister, loyal cousin and friend, as well as destroying her image of herself as child, she becomes, in a social sense, a person without an identity. Maggie's childhood self-definition conflicts, after her elopement, with society's expectations. From her childhood, Maggie had striven to repress her intelligence and aspirations in order to "make a ball" of herself and slip into the "round hole" of her family's expectations. Her functionalised view of herself as daughter and sister prevented her from exploring alternate and expanded avenues of self-definition. Now, as an alien, functionless being in a hostile society, there is only one refuge for Maggie: the return to the safe, sure identity of early childhood which death alone makes possible.

DOROTHEA BROOKE

George Eliot introduces Dorothea Brooke as a young lady who is "enamoured of intensity and greatness, and rash in embracing whatever seemed to her to have those aspects; likely to seek martyrdom, to make retractions, and then to incur martyrdom after all in a quarter where she had not sought it." (M, 6) This description of Dorothea's character prophetically charts the complex process of her search for her self-definition. As an unmarried young lady, Dorothea courts a sort of martyrdom: her refusal to fulfill the conventional stereotyped roles of Middlemarch society renders her vulnerable to social criticism and scorn. Dorothea's decision to marry Edward Casaubon is a personal "retraction" of martyrdom, for she hopes to find self-fulfillment and happiness in her marriage. Ironically, this marriage is the very "quarter" in which Dorothea unexpectedly incurs real martyrdom: the duties of her married life threaten to annihilate her sense of selfhood just as surely as physical martyrdom extinguishes the life of the victim.

Prior to her marriage, Dorothea defines herself chiefly by negation. Her aspirations are indefinite and vague; she knows only that she "yearns after some lofty conception of the world which might frankly include the parish of Tipton and her own rule of conduct there." (*M*, 6) Although the young Dorothea does not know precisely what she wants to be, she has decidedly fixed notions about the roles which she will not perform. Like Elizabeth Bennet, Dorothea rejects the roles of daughter, sister and potential wife. Unlike Elizabeth, Emma and Maggie, Dorothea has no living parents whose existence offers her the socially acceptable definition of herself as daughter. In Mr. Brooke, her uncle and guardian, Dorothea does have a sort of father-figure. Mr. Brooke, in his ineffectuality and lack of guiding principles, resembles Mr. Bennet and Mr. Woodhouse. Although he is less eccentric than the latter, Mr. Brooke's confused mental state is somewhat akin to Mr. Woodhouse's:

> *It was hardly a year since they [Dorothea and Celia] had come to live at Tipton Grange with their uncle [Mr. Brooke], a man nearly sixty, of acquiescent temper, miscellaneous opinions, and uncertain vote. He had travelled in his younger years, and was held in this part of the country to have contracted a too rambling habit of mind. Mr. Brooke's conclusions were as difficult to predict as the weather; it was only safe to say that he would act with benevolent intentions, and that he would spend as little money as possible in carrying them out.* (M, 6)

Like Mr. Bennet, Mr. Brooke fails to fulfill the paternal obligations which accrue to his role as guardian. His delicate ego and his uneasiness in dealing with members of the opposite sex cause him to abdicate much of his parental authority to Dorothea:

> *These peculiarities of Dorothea's character [her ardent religiosity] caused Mr. Brooke to be all the more blamed in neighbouring families for not securing some middle-aged lady as guide and companion to his nieces. But he himself dreaded so much the superior sort of woman likely to be available for such a position, that he allowed himself to be dissuaded by Dorothea's objections, . . . So Miss Brooke presided in her uncle's household, and did not at all dislike her new authority, with the homage that belonged to it.* (M, 8)

90

On a superficial level, Dorothea's position as the novel opens appears to be almost identical to Emma's. Both heroines enjoy a position of considerable personal freedom because of the absence of effective parental guidance and both enjoy the social prestige which accrues to the position of mistress of the household. The great difference between Emma and Dorothea inheres in the way in which each heroine responds to her situation. Since Emma's society offers her no constructive scope for the exercise of her intelligence and imagination, she channels these qualities into a socially destructive desire to dominate; Emma cleverly exploits her function as daughter and mistress of Hartfield in order to fulfill her aspirations to power. Unlike Emma's concrete and social ambitions, Dorothea's aspirations are largely theoretical, idealized and unarticulated. Her social function as Mr. Brooke's ward and mistress of his home serves to frustrate, rather than to fulfill, her aspirations. Moreover, Dorothea's moral sensitivity and sincerity would, in any case, prevent her from adopting the deceptive stance which Emma so frequently employs.

Although her social position is akin to Emma's Dorothea's real dilemma most clearly resembles Elizabeth Bennet's. Dorothea's intelligence prevents her from identifying with her role as niece, but her moral sense of family loyalty compels her to participate in her familial society. Dorothea and Elizabeth, because of their sensitivity, cannot detach themselves from their family circle with the aplomb which Emma Woodhouse displays.

Mr. Brooke's behavior and values do not approach the offensive vulgarity which characterizes Mrs. Bennet's. Nevertheless, his conduct causes the sensitive Dorothea the same kind of embarrassment which Elizabeth suffers from her mother's social comportment. Mr. Brooke offends Dorothea's sense of social justice. Her ardent concern for the state of the cottagers on her uncle's estate contrasts sharply with Mr. Brooke's indifference:

> "I think we deserve to be beaten out of our beautiful houses
> with a scourge of small cords--all of us who let tenants live
> in such sties as we see around us." (M, 23)

Mr. Brooke's laissez-faire social attitude frustrates Dorothea's desire for social justice and makes her incapable of that inward deference to authority which her social function demands:

> In Mr. Brooke the hereditary strain of Puritan energy was in

abeyance; but in his niece Dorothea it glowed alike through faults and virtues, turning sometimes into impatience of her uncle's talk or his way of "letting things be" on his estate, and making her long all the more for the time when she would be of age and have some command of money for generous schemes. (M, 6)

Just as Mr. Brooke's social insensitivity offends Dorothea's moral sense of justice, his "too rambling habit of mind" affronts her intellectual acuity. When Mr. Casaubon comes to dine for the first time, Dorothea correctly assesses Mr. Brooke's conversation as trivial; she is embarrassed for her uncle's sake and fearful of the effect which her uncle's innate garrulousness will have upon the esteemed Mr. Casaubon. Mr. Brooke adds insult to injury when he proceeds to denigrate Dorothea's intelligence in the presence of Mr. Casaubon. When Dorothea ventures to express her views, her comments are dismissed with the condescension which male society reserves for female opinion: "Young ladies don't understand political economy, you know," said Mr. Brooke, smiling towards Mr. Casaubon (*M*, 12); "No, no," said Mr. Brooke, shaking his head, "I cannot let young ladies meddle with my documents. Young ladies are too flighty." (*M*, 14)

Mr. Brooke is not consciously cruel to Dorothea. He is simply incapable of understanding women except in terms of generalized sexist stereotypes. Moreover, he is intimidated by aggressive women, like Mrs. Cadwallader, and by intelligent women, like Dorothea herself. His limited vision, intellectual impercipience and social irresponsibility make it impossible for Dorothea to respect him and to define herself in terms of her role as his niece. But, like Elizabeth Bennet, Dorothea refrains from open criticism and affords her uncle the outward deference to which his position entitles him.

Dorothea cannot wholeheartedly define herself as Mr. Brooke's niece, nor can she fulfill the role of sister to Celia. Dorothea and Celia do not perform the reciprocal sisterly functions which Mrs. Ellis describes. Dorothea can hardly unfold "her own store of painful experience" to her sister. Indeed, she evades Celia's questions about her honeymoon in Rome: "No one would ever know what she thought of a wedding journey to Rome." (*M*, 204) Nor can Dorothea achieve the sense of self-repression where "Self becomes as nothing in comparison with the intense interest excited by a sister's experience."[14] Dorothea, because of her need for energetic self-assertion, is unable to fulfill the role of the doting aunt which Emma exploits so well. After Mr. Casaubon's death, Dorothea visits Celia at Freshitt, but she soon wearies of the idle function of the adoring aunt:

> *After three months Freshitt had become rather oppressive: to sit like a model for Saint Catherine looking rapturously at Celia's baby would not do for many hours in the day, and to remain in that momentous babe's presence with persistent disregard was a course that could not have been tolerated in a childless sister. Dorothea would have been capable of carrying baby joyfully for a mile if there had been need, and of loving it the more tenderly for that labour; but to an aunt who does not recognize her infant nephew as Bouddha, and has nothing to do for him but to admire, his behaviour is apt to appear monotonous, and the interest of watching him exhaustible.* (M, 390)

Dorothea's refusal to define herself as the childless aunt was prepared for in earlier scenes between herself and Celia. It is not a moral flaw, as in the case of Elizabeth and Lydia Bennet, which separates Dorothea and Celia but, rather, a difference in vision. Celia's practical unimaginative vision is as far removed from Dorothea's theoretic idealistic vision as the "criticisms of Murr the Cat" are from "us beings of wider speculation." When Eliot implicitly compares Celia to "Murr the Cat" she points out that Celia's vision is on a less exalted level than Dorothea's. It does not necessarily follow, however, that Celia's perception is inaccurate or that her observations are unjust:

> *"You always see what nobody else sees; it is impossible to satisfy you; yet you never see what is quite plain. That's your way, Dodo." Something certainly gave Celia unusual courage; and she was not sparing the sister of whom she was occasionally in awe. Who can tell what just criticisms Murr the Cat may be passing on us beings of wider speculation.* (M, 27)

It is unfortunate for Dorothea that she cannot bring herself to take Celia seriously. Although Celia's vision is often mundane, she has an intuitive insight into Dorothea's motivation. Celia recognizes the repressive excesses of Dorothea's asceticism and she instinctively perceives the illusory nature of Dorothea's view of Mr. Casaubon.

Essentially, Dorothea cannot function as Celia's sister because she is unable to feel that "intense interest" in Celia's "experience" which Mrs. Ellis describes as characterizing the proper sisterly relationship. Celia is interested in conventional things: music, jewelry, pretty clothes and, most of all, marriage. Celia is happy to consider herself as a potential wife, as her society expects, while Dorothea defiantly rejects this stereotyped role.

The first chapter of *Middlemarch* describes society's opinion of Dorothea and Celia and illustrates the degree to which young ladies are defined according to their function as potential wives. Dorothea's intellectual and religious ardor is meaningful to her society only as it affects her prospects for marriage: "Certainly such elements in the character of a marriageable girl tended to interfere with her lot, and hinder it from being decided according to custom, by good looks, vanity, and merely canine affection." (*M*, 6) Society defines Dorothea as an attractive marital prospect, in appearance and fortune, with this one reservation:

> *And how should Dorothea not marry? --a girl so handsome and with such prospects? Nothing could hinder it but her love of extremes, and her insistance on regulating life according to notions which might cause a wary man to hesitate before he made her an offer, or might even lead her at last to refuse all offers . . . Women were expected to have weak opinions; but the great safeguard of society and of domestic life was, that opinions were not acted on. Sane people did what their neighbours did; so that if any lunatics were at large, one might know and avoid them.* (M, 7)

Dorothea's society does not criticize her "strange whims of fasting like a Papist, and of sitting up at night to read old theological books" (*M*, 7) largely because women's private religious ideas are considered to be insignificant. The real criticism which society levels is directed at Dorothea's unconventional refusal to display the stereotyped interests and attributes expected of a potential wife.

Dorothea displays a most unconventional indifference to Sir James Chettam's romantic attentions. She disdainfully declines his offer of a riding horse and his gallantly conventional gift of a Maltese puppy. The latter gift was prompted by

94

Sir James' generalized belief that "ladies are usually fond of these Maltese dogs." (M, 22) Indeed, Dorothea is interested in Sir James only when he appeals to her intelligence and unconventional social aspirations. Dorothea considers Sir James to be a fine partner in the business of planning cottages, but his gallant compliments and gestures serve only to perplex and annoy her.

Dorothea says more than she realizes when she tells Sir James "I am rather short-sighted." Her inability to realize that Sir James is actually courting her displays the limited vision which Celia remarks in her. Dorothea appears to be insensitive to Sir James when she is really acting according to her limited child-like view of marriage:

> *Dorothea, with all her eagerness to know the truths of life, retained very childlike ideas about marriage. She felt sure that she would have accepted the judicious Hooker, if she had been born in time to save him from that wretched mistake he made in matrimony; or John Milton when his blindness had come on; or any of the other great men whose odd habits it would have been a glorious piety to endure; but an amiable baronet, who said "Exactly" to her remarks even when she expressed uncertainty,--how could he affect her as a lover? The really delightful marriage must be that where your husband was a sort of father, and could teach you even Hebrew, if you wished it. (M, 7-8)*

Dorothea's ideas about marriage reveal that she has, at this point, no theoretical objection to achieving her self-definition through her husband. Indeed her ideal husband will offer her a sense of identity by affording her an opportunity to exercise her piety and her intelligence. What Dorothea does object to however, is the idea of marriage to a conventional, socially acceptable gentleman who will offer her only a conventional stereotyped self-definition. Sir James, who represents the epitome of conventionality, is thus automatically excluded from Dorothea's consideration. She assumes that he must really be in love with the equally conventional Celia. When Celia informs Dorothea that she is the real object of Sir James' attentions and implies that Sir James has interpreted Dorothea's interest in his cottage plans as a sign of affection, Dorothea reacts with anger and disgust. Dorothea had imagined that Sir James respected her intelligence and her social aspirations; it comes as a heavy blow when she realizes that Sir James has merely humored what Celia calls her "fad" for drawing plans. In her disappointment, Dorothea refuses to admit her own error in judgment. Instead, she blames the limitations of her society:

> *Dorothea was too much jarred to recover her temper and*
> *behave so as to show that she admitted any error in herself.*
> *She was disposed rather to accuse the intolerable narrowness*
> *and the purblind conscience of the society around her: . . .*
> *The* fad *of drawing plans! What was life worth--what great*
> *faith was possible when the whole effect of one's actions*
> *could be withered up into such parched rubbish as that?*
> (M, 27)

Dorothea feels that her society offers her no opportunity for achieving a satisfactory sense of self-definition. When she resolves to marry Mr. Casaubon, Dorothea is aware that society will disapprove of her choice: "Of course all the world round Tipton would be out of sympathy with this marriage. Dorothea knew of no one who thought as she did about life and its best objects." (*M*, 36)

Dorothea looks to Mr. Casaubon to establish an identity for her and to provide her with a fulfilling self-definition. She is blind to the fact that Mr. Casaubon's expectations for a wife are fully as conventional as those of Sir James Chettam. Dorothea fancies that Mr. Casaubon desires a partner and companion with whom he can share his intellectual endeavors. Instead, Mr. Casaubon really wants his wife to be a self-sacrificing, adoring, ornamental diversion:

> *But he had deliberately incurred the hindrance [of court-*
> *ship], having made up his mind that it was now time for him*
> *to adorn his life with the graces of female companionship,*
> *to irradiate the gloom which fatigue was apt to hang over the*
> *intervals of studious labour with the play of female fancy,*
> *and to secure in this, his culminating age, the solace of*
> *female tendance for his declining years.* (M, 46)

Despite the disapproval of Middlemarch society, the only thing which is even faintly unconventional in the marriage of Dorothea and Mr. Casaubon is the disparity in their ages. Mr. Casaubon's expectations for his future wife harmonize perfectly with the stereotyped functions assigned to women since the eighteenth century:

The eighteenth century education of girls intended to pro-
duce bodily and mental debility. The vital principle is that
the girl is to be brought up as a companion for a man, not,
however, a companion who will share in his serious occupa-
tions and strengthen him in his daily work, but a companion
who shall never offend his vanity by any display of knowl-
edge or wisdom.[15]

Dorothea has so seriously deceived herself that it is inevitable that her married
life should bring a series of disappointments. She had imagined that she would
find a satisfactory self-definition "though only as a lamp-holder" to Mr. Casaubon. (M, 13) But, at the same time, she had expected that Mr. Casaubon
would provide her with other, larger opportunities for self-definition. She
imagined that her collaboration in his work would make her "wise" and there-
by enable her to pursue her private plans for cottage building: "He [Mr.
Casaubon] would not disapprove of her occupying herself with it [cottage
building] in leisure moments, as other women expected to occupy themselves
with their dress and embroidery." (M, 25)

The greatest disappointment which her marriage brings to Dorothea is the
realization that Mr. Casaubon does not value her for herself, but only in terms
of her function as his wife:

She was always trying to be what her husband wished, and
never able to repose on his delight in what she was. The
thing that she liked, that she spontaneously cared to have,
seemed to be always excluded from her life; for if it was
only granted and not shared by her husband it might as well
have been denied. (M, 348. Emphasis added.)

Dorothea's ceaseless efforts to suppress her own aspirations and needs in order
to please her husband result, as we have seen, in the virtual annihilation of her
own identity. As is the case with Maggie, Dorothea's self-image and self-definition merge under the influence of another's dominant personality. Even Dorothea's speech patterns reflect her loss of a sense of individuality. After her
marriage she uses almost no figurative language and more rhetorical questions.
Derek Oldfield has noted how this change in Dorothea's manner of self-expres-
sion is "a dramatization of someone dangerously isolated, affirming her values
out loud in an effort to keep a grip on them."[16] Dorothea loses that ontological sense of being of which Marcel speaks; she comes to see herself as a crea-

ical sense of being of which Marcel speaks: she comes to see herself as a creature submerged by her function.

During the course of her marriage, Dorothea gradually assumes the functionalised existence which Mr. Casaubon expects of her. She suppresses her former intellectual aspirations and becomes the subservient kind of helpmate which her husband had originally sought in marriage--"such a helpmate to him as would enable him to dispense with a hired secretary." (*M*, 205)

In addition to repressing her intellectual aspirations, Dorothea also represses her spontaneity. When watching Mr. Featherstone's funeral, Dorothea energetically expresses herself but she recedes into silence at her husband's appearance:

> *"How piteous!" said Dorothea. "This funeral seems to me the most dismal thing I ever saw. It is a blot on the morning. I cannot bear to think that any one should die and leave no love behind."*
> *She was going to say more, but she saw her husband enter and seat himself a little in the background. The difference his presence made to her was not always a happy one: she felt that he often inwardly objected to her speech.* (M, 240)

The artificiality and lack of spontaneity which characterize Dorothea's relationship to her husband is a natural result of the functionalised existence which marriage imposed upon the nineteenth century woman:

> *A wife could charm her husband, or coax him, or vex him, but she could never employ reason; it was not in the bond. She found herself never entirely natural in his presence, never wholly frank, for she never wholly knew him; and it dawned upon her that perhaps he never wholly knew her.*[17]

When Will Ladislaw objects to Dorothea's isolated, repressive existence, Dorothea responds in terms of her function as a wife:

> *"But you may easily carry the help too far," he [Will] said, "and get overwrought yourself. Are you not too much shut up? You already look paler. It would be better for Mr. Casaubon to have a secretary."*

"How can you think of that?" said Dorothea, in a tone of earnest remonstrance. "I should have no happiness if I did not help him in his work. What could I do? There is no good to be done in Lowick. The only thing I desire is to help him more." (M, 267)

Dorothea's functionalised existence has isolated her from her society and blunted her ardent social concern. Once she had scorned the idea "that a young lady of fortune should find her ideal of life in village charities, patronage of the humbler clergy, the perusal of 'Female Scripture Characters' . . . and the care of her own soul over her embroidery in her own boudoir." (M, 21) But now, as a married woman of fortune, Dorothea's social awareness is even more limited than the stereotyped ideal which she had formerly rejected:

Dorothea seldom left home without her husband, but she did occasionally drive into Middlemarch alone, on little errands of shopping or charity such as occur to every lady of wealth when she lives within three miles of a town. (M, 315)

Her isolation from the human community has had a depersonalizing effect upon Dorothea. When she is released from the grasp of Casaubon's "dead hand" Dorothea achieves a healthy self-definition in terms of the human family. In perceiving that "the objects of her rescue were not to be sought out by her fancy, they were chosen for her" Dorothea realizes that her self-definition derives, not from the identity of any one person but from the strength of her own generous and ardently loving nature. (M, 577)

JANE EYRE

The potentially depersonalizing effects of "functionalism" are perhaps most dramatically illustrated in Jane Eyre's struggle for self-definition. Like Dorothea Brooke and Elizabeth Bennet, Jane is unable to identify with the dominant parental figures in her life. As a young child, Jane's positive self-image causes her to reject the dehumanizing assessments of her character which Mrs. Reed and Mr. Brocklehurst attempt to impose upon her. Jane, like Dorothea, Elizabeth and Emma, also rejects the definition of herself as a potential wife.

Janes' search for self-definition is, in many ways, more complicated than that

of any of the other talented heroines. In addition to the functionalised definition of herself as an obedient niece and a potential wife, Jane's society defines
her in terms of her social role as governess. The other talented heroines must
struggle with social definitions which are too limited in scope to permit their
achieving self-fulfillment. Nevertheless, their societies do offer them some sense
of identity; their dilemma consists largely in deciding whether they shall accept
or reject the inadequate and limited scope which their societies provide. The
role of governess which society assigns to Jane Eyre fails to offer even an
inadequate sense of self-definition. The nineteenth century governess was, by
definition, a being without an identity.

The Victorian governess has been described as "a broken-spirited, submissive
dependent."[18] A writer in the *Quarterly Review* pointed out the cruelties of
the governess's anomalous social position:

> *The real definition of a governess, in the English sense, is*
> *a being who is our equal in birth, manners, and education,*
> *but our inferior in worldly wealth. Take a lady, in every*
> *meaning of the word, born and bred, and let her father pass*
> *through the* Gazette *[declare bankruptcy], and she wants*
> *nothing more to suit our highest* beau ideal *of a guide and*
> *instructress to our children. We need the imprudencies,*
> *extravagances, mistakes, or crimes of a certain number of*
> *fathers to sow that seed from which we reap the harvest of*
> *governesses. There is no other class which so cruelly requires*
> *its members to be, in birth, mind, and manners, above their*
> *station, in order to fit them for their station.*[19]

The governess was neither a servant nor a member of the family. Since she held
no fixed position on the social scale, members of society found her presence
both confusing and unpleasant:

> *She is a bore to almost any gentleman, as a tabooed woman,*
> *to whom he is interdicted from granting the usual privileges*
> *of the sex, and yet who is perpetually crossing his path. She*
> *is a bore to most ladies by the same rule, and a reproach, too*
> *--for her dull, fagging, bread-and-water life is perpetually*
> *putting their pampered listlessness to shame. The servants*
> *invariably detest her, for she is a dependent like themselves,*

*and yet, for all that, as much their superior in other respects
as the family they both serve. Her pupils may love her, and
she may take the deepest interest in them, but they cannot
be her friends.*[20]

The governess was, in a sense, a creature without a social past and without a
future. A young woman became a governess for one of two reasons. Either, like
Maggie Tulliver, she was in a position of financial distress or, like Jane Eyre,
she had no relatives who could support her or give her a home. Whether she
were an orphan or a member of an indigent family, the governess was denied
the sense of "being" which comes from having socially recognized origins.
Polite middle-class society viewed financial need and the lack of good connections almost as embarrassing obscenities. Good taste dictated that the governess's former situation never be referred to; she was not to be thought of in terms
of her personal past. Rather, she was the disembodied, depersonalized "lady"
whose function was to teach the children of the middle and upper classes.
Just as the governess was deprived of her sense of a personal past, she was also
denied the opportunity of attaining a socially acceptable middle-class identity
as a wife. She was a "tabooed" woman to any gentleman because she was not
his social equal. Yet, as a "lady" she could not fraternize with male members
of the servant class.

The other talented heroines, Elizabeth Bennet, Emma Woodhouse, Dorothea
Brooke and Maggie Tulliver, are depersonalized by their societies precisely
because of their sexuality and the stereotyped expectations which accrue to
the condition of being female. Jane Eyre, by virtue of her function as governess, is denied even the recognition of her sexuality. The governess, living and
working in a family's home, was inevitably brought into contact with the male
members of the household. If she were a reasonably attractive woman, she was
obviously a potential source of temptation to the men and a threat to the
women of the home. In order to reduce this sexual tension, elaborate codes of
behavior were established for the purpose of reducing the governess's existence as a sexual being. Every courtesy, attraction or flirtation between a
gentleman and a governess was forbidden, ostensibly because of the disparity
of their social situations.[21] Yet, the governess's status as a "lady" was adduced
to prevent gentlemen from seeing her as an object for sexual dalliance: "Physical relations with a woman of the working class seem to have caused no social
obligations, while sexual relations with a woman so nearly of one's own class
could not be isolated from a whole complex of responsibilities."[22]

Despite the social attempt to desexualize and depersonalize the governess, the social code was sometimes breached:

> *In some instances . . . the love of admiration has led the governess to try and make herself necessary to the comfort of the father of the family in which she resided, and by delicate and unnoticed flattery gradually to gain her point, to the disparagement of the mother, and the destruction of mutual happiness. When the latter was homely, or occupied with domestic cares, opportunity was found to bring forward attractive accomplishments, or by sedulous attentions to supply her lack of them; or the sons were in some instances objects of notice and flirtation, or when occasion offered, visitors at the house.*
>
> *This kind of conduct has led to the inquiry which is frequently made before engaging an instructress, "Is she handsome or attractive?" If so, it is conclusive against her.*[23]

From this fear of the governess's sexuality derived the stereotyped notion that the good governess should be a homely, severe, unfeminine type of woman.[24]

The talented heroines, with the exception of Maggie and Jane, are not forced to assume the undesirable function of the governess. But most of the talented heroines, directly or indirectly, come in contact with young women who are compelled to fulfill the barely respectable social role of the governess. Lady Catherine De Bourgh exhibits her society's functionalised view of the governess in *Pride and Prejudice*. She boasts of her social power by describing her ability to "supply" good families with that necessary commodity--a governess.

> *"It is wonderful how many families I have been the means of supplying in that way. I am always glad to get a young person well placed out . . . Mrs. Collins, did I tell you of Lady Metcalfe's calling yesterday to thank me? She finds Miss Pope a treasure. 'Lady Catherine,' said she, 'you have given me a treasure.' "* (P & P, 125)

Jane Fairfax, in *Emma*, is aware of the loss of identity which her future role as governess will entail. She thinks of the position of governess, with its requirement of total self-effacement, as analogous to the religious life:

102

She had long resolved that one-and-twenty should be the
period [of beginning to earn her living]. With the fortitude
of a devoted noviciate, she had resolved at one-and-twenty
to complete the sacrifice, and retire from all the pleasures
of life, of rational intercourse, equal society, peace and hope,
to penance and mortification forever. (E, 110)

Maggie Tulliver uses animal imagery to describe the limited, depersonalized existence of her two years in a dreary schoolroom:

"It is with me as I used to think it would be with the poor
uneasy white bear I saw at the show. I thought he must have
got so stupid with the habit of turning backwards and
forwards in that narrow space, that he would keep doing it
if they set him free. One gets a bad habit of being unhappy."
(MF, 325)

Mary Garth's Middlemarch society treats governesses as objects of scorn and ridicule. The Vincy family's governess, Miss Morgan, appears to Rosamund's condescending eye to be "just the sort of person for a governess" since, while everything about her is "blooming and joyous," Miss Morgan alone appears "brown, dull, and resigned." (M, 120) Rosamund's mother considers Mary Garth to be "a dreadful plain girl--more fit for a governess." (M, 76) In light of the impersonal way in which her society views its governesses, it is no wonder that the high-spirited Mary Garth prefers the relative independence of nursing the cantankerous Mr. Featherstone.

Jane Eyre welcomes the chance to open her own school because this humble job provides her with an opportunity for self-definition:

Diana and Mary were soon to leave Moor House, and return
to the far different life and scene which awaited them, as
governesses in a large, fashionable, south-of-England city;
where each held a situation in families, by whose wealthy
and haughty members they were regarded only as humble
dependents, and who neither knew nor sought one of their
innate excellences, and appreciated only their acquired
accomplishments as they appreciated the skill of their cook
or the taste of their waiting-woman. (JE, 310)

During Mr. Rochester's house party, the imperious Blanche Ingram amuses the assembled company by relating how she and her sister and brother enjoyed tormenting their governesses. Blanche's society views such creatures as mere objects; Blanche vents her cruel opinions despite the fact that Jane is present in the room:

> *"I have just one word to say of the whole tribe [of govern-*
> *esses]; they are a nuisance. Not that I ever suffered much*
> *from them; I took care to turn the tables. What tricks Theo-*
> *dore and I used to play on our Miss Wilsons, and Mrs. Greys,*
> *and Madame Jouberts! . . . The best fun was with Madame*
> *Joubert. Miss Wilson was a poor sickly thing, lachrymose and*
> *low-spirited: not worth the trouble of vanquishing, in short;*
> *and Mrs. Grey was coarse and insensible: no blow took effect*
> *on her. But poor Madame Joubert! I see her yet in her*
> *raging passions, when we had driven her to extremities--*
> *spilt our tea, crumbled our bread and butter, tossed our*
> *books up to the ceiling, and played a charivari with the*
> *ruler and desk, the fender and fire-irons. Theodore, do you*
> *remember those merry days?'* (JE, 155-156)

The Victorian governess, in fact and fiction, was truly submerged by her function. Deprived of her past, denied any hopes for a better future, her very existence as a woman was negated since it interfered with the proper execution of her function. In light of all of this, one would expect Jane Eyre, poor, orphaned and homely, to exhibit the "brown, dull, and resigned" demeanor which characterized the Vincy's Miss Morgan. Indeed, it is remarkable that Jane can even be considered in a chapter which is concerned with self-definition. Jane's social world has conspired, it would appear, to deprive her of her sexuality, her identity, and any opportunity for self-definition. According to stereotyped social expectation, Jane, as a governess, "had no social position worthy of attention. She was at best unenvied and at worst the object of mild scorn, and all she sought was survival in genteel obscurity."[25]

Jane's sense of self-esteem, her intelligence and her aspiring nature prevent her from accepting the demeaning, functionalised definition which society reserves for governesses. Jane's unconventional attitude towards her pupil Adele distinguishes her from the stereotyped ideal of the governess as the uncritical willing slave of her charges. Jane rather critically assesses Adele as a "spoilt and indulged" child who is therefore "sometimes wayward." (*JE*, 94) Aware that her reasoned view of Adele is unconventional, Jane offers the following explanation:

> *This . . . will be thought cool language by persons who entertain solemn doctrines about the angelic nature of children, and the duty of those charged with their education to conceive for them an idolatrous devotion: but I am not writing to flatter parental egotism, to echo cant, or prop up humbug. I am merely telling the truth.* (JE, 95)

In her relationship with Mr. Rochester, Jane departs even more flagrantly from the stereotyped requirements of her function. Her spirited self-assertion towards her master reveals that Jane is anything but a "broken-spirited, submissive dependent."[26] Jane's morally sensitive nature rebels at the notion that Mr. Rochester's social position indicates his innate superiority to herself:

> *"I don't think, sir, you have a right to command me merely because you are older than I, or because you have seen more of the world than I have; your claim to superiority depends on the use you have made of your time and experience."* (JE, 118)

Jane even dares to invert the traditional master-servant relationship. She assumes a stance of moral superiority when she lectures Rochester on the necessity of improving the moral tenor of his life:

> *"You said you were not as good as you would like to be, and that you regretted your own imperfection; . . . you intimated that to have a sullied memory was a perpetual bane. It seems to me, that if you tried hard, you would in time find it possible to become what you yourself would approve; and that if from this day you began with resolution to correct your thoughts and actions, you would in a few years have laid up a new and stainless store of recollections; to which you might revert with pleasure."* (JE, 121)

Jane's willingness to listen to the sorry tale of Rochester's past life illustrates how she spontaneously relates to him as a person instead of in terms of established social roles. This indication of Jane's moral sensitivity affronted the conventional sensibilities of nineteenth century readers:

> *In the* Quarterly Review, *Jane Eyre was branded as vulgar-minded and Rochester was censored because he poured into Jane's ears "disgraceful tales of his past life, connected with the birth of little Adele, which any man with common decency and respect for a woman, and that a mere girl of eighteen, would have spared her . . ."*[27]

When Jane falls in love with Rochester, before he declares his love for her, she violates two of the most strongly established social rules of her society. She fails to assume the passive role which Dr. Gregory recommends to young ladies:

> *Though a woman has no reason to be ashamed of an attachment to a man of merit, yet Nature, whose authority is superior to philosophy, has annexed a sense of shame to it. It is even long before a woman of delicacy dares to avow to her own heart that she loves; and when all the subterfuges of ingenuity to conceal it from herself fail, she feels a violence done both to her pride and to her modesty. . . .*
> *It is a maxim laid down among you, and a very prudent one it is, that love is not to begin on your part, but is entirely to be the consequence of our attachment to you.*[28]

Jane certainly fails to feel the requisite sense of shame because of her love for Rochester. Indeed, she herself, as he later reminds her, actually takes the initiative in proposing marriage. (*JE*, 230)

When Jane and Rochester become formally engaged, Jane faces a dilemma which she shares with Elizabeth Bennet, Emma, and Dorothea Brooke: she finds it impossible to define herself as a potential wife. Actually this dilemma is one which, according to social expectations, should not confront Jane at all. Her society defines Jane in terms of her function as governess and this role demands that she suppress her identity as a sexual being. In daring to feel passion for her master and openly asserting her love, Jane defies the social codes which would desexualize and depersonalize her.

During the period of courtship, Jane resents Rochester's attempt to adorn her with the elaborate finery of a fashionable lady. She correctly interprets his efforts to alter her outward appearance as a sign of his desire to impose an artificial, conventional self-definition upon her. When Rochester takes her shopping for a trousseau, Jane feels only rebellion; she realizes that her function as governess is soon to be replaced by the equally repressive social role of the ornamental wife:

> *Glad was I to get him out of the silk warehouse, and then out of a jeweller's shop: the more he bought me, the more my cheek burned with a sense of annoyance and degradation . . . "It would, indeed, be a relief," I thought, "if I had ever so small an independency; I never can bear being dressed like a doll by Mr. Rochester, or sitting like a second Danae with the golden shower falling daily round me." (JE, 236)*

Like Dorothea Brooke, Jane wishes her future husband to respect her personal sense of being, to be able to "repose on his delight in what she was." (M, 348) When Rochester defines her in terms of the conventional, stereotyped ideal of the woman as angel, Jane proudly asserts her individuality:

> *"I am not an angel," I asserted; "and I will not be one till I die: I will be myself. Mr. Rochester, you must neither expect nor exact anything celestial of me--for you will not get it." (JE, 228)*

Rochester's attempt to impose a new and alien self-definition upon Jane is illustrated through the suggestive use of the wedding veil. Jane has made a veil for her wedding which harmonizes with her own self-image. She has chosen a plain "square of unembroidered blond" [silk lace formed in hexagonal meshes] and explains to Rochester that she deems this to be a proper covering for her "low-born head" since she can bring her husband "neither fortune, beauty, nor connections." (JE, 247) The choice of a modest head-covering is not a sign of self-abasement on Jane's part. Rather, it demonstrates the preference for simplicity and sincerity which characterizes her nature and her personality

The extravagant, costly wedding veil which Rochester purchases for Jane seems, to her, to symbolize a sort of deception and artificiality in their relationship as lovers. She interprets his gift as an indication of his desire to disguise her true nature: "I smiled as I unfolded it, and devised how I would tease you [Rochester] about your aristocratic tastes, and your efforts to masque your plebian bride in the attributes of a princess." (*JE*, 247) Appropriately, it is this costly veil which Bertha Rochester destroys in a fit of insane rage. Rochester's silence about Bertha's existence constitutes his grossest act of deception against Jane. When Bertha tears the veil her action symbolically predicts the failure of Rochester's attempts at deception. Jane will discover the secret which her lover has hidden from her, and this discovery will cause her categorically to reject the artificial and dishonest self-definition which Rochester offers her.

When Jane dresses for her wedding, she wears the plain veil which she herself had chosen. In a sense, her retention of this modest article indicates her refusal to surrender her independent identity. Yet, when Jane observes her image in a mirror, she feels a sudden loss of identity: "I saw a robed and veiled figure, so unlike my usual self that it seemed almost the image of a stranger." (*JE*, 252) At this moment, Jane realizes that she is in danger of losing her unique sense of being. She feels that, in acting an alien role, she is a stranger to herself. In her mirror Jane beholds a functionalised creature--the ornamental bride of a wealthy gentleman. It is a self-definition which she instinctively rejects, but her love for Rochester and her ignorance of his deception prevent her from acting upon the basis of this intuitive realization.

As it does with Elizabeth, Emma, and Dorothea, self-knowledge eventually adjusts Jane's self-image and her self-definition. When the fact of Rochester's former marriage is revealed. Jane recognizes how she had almost deluded herself into accepting a false self-definition. Like Elizabeth and Emma, she reproaches herself for her lack of insight: "Oh, how blind had been my eyes! How weak my conduct!" (*JE*, 260)

The options for self-definition which Rochester offers Jane are all unsuitable in terms of Jane's unique and aspiring character. His initial offer of marriage provides Jane with an opportunity to achieve a social status which is superficially desirable but which is based upon deception and dishonesty. Such a marriage would ultimately erode the candor, simplicity and sincerity which comprise Jane's unique personality.

As their relationship during their engagement indicates, Jane's marriage to Rochester would also be debilitating in another, more personal way. Rochester not only offers a union based upon deception, but he also proposes the kind of marital relationship which would reduce Jane to a "mere assemblage of functions."[29] For all his Byronic unconventionality, Rochester is a prisoner of his society's limited and stereotyped view of women. During their brief courtship, he treats Jane with the conventional possessiveness and superficial gallantry which had marked his relationships with his former mistresses. Jane is, to Rochester, an object to adorn and a possession which he hopes to display with pride. Despite Jane's protests--"I will not be your English Celine Varens" (*JE*, 237)--Rochester clearly intends to reduce Jane's existence to the ornamental, depersonalized function of "the angel in the house."

In a very real sense, truth is the means by which Jane is set free. Her rejection of Rochester's final offer--to define herself as his mistress--is only possible because Jane has retained a self-definition which is independent of her former function of governess and of the proferred functions of fiance, wife, and finally, mistress. This independent sense of selfhood, which her passion for Rochester threatens but never destroys, derives from Jane's providential *Weltanschauung*. She has seen herself, since her days at Lowood, as a child of God. It is this self-definition which gives Jane the courage and independence to leave Rochester despite her great love for him. Her sense of herself as a child of God in an ordered providential universe constitutes the "preconceived opinions, forgone determinations" to which she clings in her time of temptation. Jane "plants her foot" upon the immutable rock of Divine Providence:

> "I will hold to the principles received by me when I was sane, and not mad--as I am now. Laws and principles are not for the times when there is no temptation: they are for such moments as this, when body and soul rise in mutiny against their rigour; stringent are they; inviolate they shall be. If at my individual convenience I break them, what would be their worth? They have a worth--so I have always believed; and if I cannot believe it now, it is because I am insane-- quite insane: with my veins running fire, and my heart beating faster than I can count its throbs. Preconceived opinions, forgone determinations, are all I have at this hour to stand by: there I plant my foot." (JE, 279)

Jane is unique among the heroines in that the problem of self-definition is complicated by her occupation as governess. Maggie Tulliver is the only other heroine who actively works for a living, but Maggie's two year stint in a schoolroom has no demonstrable effect upon her self-definition. The problems which Jane encounters in working out her self-definition are similar to those which confront Elizabeth Bennet, Emma Woodhouse and Dorothea Brooke. All of these heroines' self-definitions are involved with the social expectations which accrue to the definition of a young lady as a submissive daughter and/or niece and a potentially obedient wife. Jane has many affinities with Elizabeth, Emma and Dorothea because the quality of her struggle involves, like theirs, a series of negations of unacceptable social definitions. But despite these numerous affinities with the other heroines, Jane most closely resembles Maggie Tulliver in her way of resolving the problem of self-definition.

Jane Eyre and Maggie Tulliver both adhere to a self-definition which is essentially unchanging. Just as Maggie consistently defines herself in terms of family loyalties, Jane Eyre retains an unaltering definition of herself as the child of a Providential Father. When they are confronted with critical choices, Jane and Maggie both base their decisions upon a self-definition which they have held from childhood. We have seen how Maggie's emotional rejection of Stephen Guest is really the logical result of defining herself according to the roles and obligations which have been imposed upon her from her youth. Similarly, Jane Eyre finds the strength to leave Mr. Rochester by turning inwards and acting in accord with the self-definition she had long adhered to.

Jane's definition of herself as a child of God is most dramatically displayed in her rejection of Rochester but it is a motif which recurs throughout the novel. When she longs for an escape from Lowood, Jane attributes her inspiration to advertise for a position to a providential intervention. When she rescues Mr. Rochester from his flaming bed, she does so by "God's aid." (*JE*, 131) After leaving Thornfield Jane wanders, destitute and isolated, among the moors. But she sees in nature a reflection of Providence and her natural refuge:

> *Not a tie holds me to human society at this moment--not a charm or hope calls me where my fellow-creatures are-- none that saw me would have a kind thought or a good wish for me. I have no relative but the universal mother, Nature: I will seek her breast and ask repose.* (JE, 284)

Jane's definition of herself in terms of Providence saved her from entering into a depersonalizing relationship with Rochester: Providence later acts to prevent Jane from choosing a repressive self-definition as St. John Rivers' wife. Jane clearly interprets the mysterious phenomenon of hearing Rochester's voice as a providential intervention on her behalf. When she and Rochester are reunited at Ferndean, Jane never tells him that she had heard his mysterious summons. But she definitely treasures the memory of this call as a sign that she is the beloved child of a Providential Father, for she applies to herself the words of the Virgin Mary: "I kept these things then, and pondered them in my heart." (*JE*, 394)

In many ways Jane Eyre is the heroine with whom the contemporary reader can most easily empathize. She earns her own living in an alien society which impersonally views her in terms of her function as a governess. The stereotyped existence of the governess with its monotonous servitude and soul-destroying anonymity is not far removed from the mechanized, depersonalized existence of Marcel's railway ticket-puncher. Jane prevails as a unique individual, despite the repressions of her society, because she defines herself in terms of being rather than in terms of doing or functioning. Her self-definition provides her with the liberty to pursue her aspirations for freedom.

All of the talented heroines aspire, in one way or another, to attain a sense of individual freedom. Their ability to realize this ambition depends upon many factors: the scope of their particular aspirations, the limitations of their societies, their own personal limitations, and the adequacy of their self-definitions. The self-definitions of the five talented heroines have been considered and assessed in terms of how well these conscious social stances allow the heroines to realize their ontological sense of being. The real test of the heroine's self-definition is the degree to which it sustains her as she strives to realize her individual aspirations.

Chapter 5

ASPIRATION AND LIMITATION

*The ontological need, the need of being, can deny itself.
. . . being and life do not coincide; my life, and by reflection
all life, may appear to me as for ever inadequate to something which I carry within me, which in a sense I am, but
which reality rejects and excludes.*[1]

This passage from Gabriel Marcel succinctly states the nature of the dilemma
which aspiration poses for the talented heroine. Each of the five heroines has
a sense of herself as an unfulfilled being who is essentially capable of living
more purposefully and "being" more profoundly than she does in actuality.
In considering the problem of self-definition, we have seen how the five talented heroines confront the reality that "being and life do not coincide." Each of
them experiences the alienation which results from the dichotomy between
"being" and "doing." Each heroine has a sense of her own inner self, or being,
and each finds that the demands of "life" in her social world not only fail to
coincide but actually conflict with her sense of her unique, personal inner
existence.

We have said that the ultimate test of the heroine's self-definition is the degree
to which it sustains her as she strives to realize her aspirations--that "something" which she carries within her but which reality "rejects and excludes."
Marcel's deliberate use of the vague term "something" is particularly appropriate to a discussion of the aspirations of the talented heroines. Most basically,
the indistinctness of "something" is applicable to the heroines because each of

them has an indistinct sense of herself as potentially capable of being something other than what she is: daughter, friend, sister, potential wife, etc. Each heroine knows that she is more than the sum of her various social functions and each of them strives to discover the intriguing "something" which she is capable of being.

On another level, the term "something," as Marcel employs it, is useful in terms of this study because it connotes a kind of complex and comprehensive way of viewing potentiality and aspiration. It is deceptively easy to catalogue and categorize the various aspirations of the five talented heroines. Using this approach, we can say that Elizabeth Bennet "aspires" to the love of Mr. Darcy, Emma Woodhouse to control and dominate, Dorothea Brooke to knowledge and heroic action, Maggie Tulliver to love, learning and beauty, and Jane Eyre to the love of Mr. Rochester. All of these observations, while correct, are in a certain sense incomplete and misleading. For this approach runs the risk of reducing the heroine to the sum of her aspirations: a result which is surely as depersonalizing as reducing her to the sum of her various functions.

Marcel's view of aspiration provides an alternative to this rather mechanized and impersonal way of seeing the heroines' aspirations. The "something" which the human person carries within herself or himself does not admit of easy classification or categorization because this "something" is part of the whole "mystery" of being. The individual human being is, in a sense, pregnant with possibilities. She or he carries her or his unique potential for life, for being, within herself or himself just as a mother carries the potential of her unborn child. Indeed, to Marcel, "being" is a mystery which defies analysis:

> *Being is what withstands--or what would withstand--an exhaustive analysis bearing on the data of experience and aiming to reduce them step by step to elements increasingly devoid of intrinsic or significant value.*[2]

However numerous the concrete ambitions and aspirations which may be assigned to each of the talented heroines, the dilemma of aspiration and limitation remains imperfectly explored unless we first realize how each heroine's aspirations stem from her desire to realize the mystery of her being and to attain the necessary freedom to create her own unique self. The heroine's need for this basic freedom is not easily fulfilled. There is a "reality" which "rejects and excludes" her sense of her own potential. Sometimes this reality may be external and take the form of social restrictions; very often, the limitations to the heroine's freedom are internal and consist of personal faults, moral flaws, or an inadequate self-definition. The heroines evince their aspirations to the basic human freedom to create oneself in various ways. In Maggie Tulliver and Dorothea Brooke, this desire for freedom manifests itself in an apparently paradoxical desire for control. In Emma Woodhouse the aspiration to be free to create has assumed the appearance of a desire to dominate. In Elizabeth Bennet and Jane Eyre the aspiration for freedom is most clearly illustrated for both heroines feel that their freedom to realize their potential can be achieved only through openly defying the web of social restraints.

Jane Eyre and Elizabeth Bennet would seem to have relatively little in common. Superficially, Elizabeth's demeanor seems incredibly subdued in comparison with the energetic unconventionality of Jane Eyre. Yet, these heroines share a positive self-image and both possess an adequate sense of self-definition. Jane's sense of herself as a child of God and Elizabeth's sense of her inherent human value are convictions which sustain them as they struggle to attain the general sense of human freedom which will permit them to realize their individual aspirations. Indeed, the self-definitions which Jane and Elizabeth have derived for themselves are so essentially healthy, so closely in harmony with the needs of their respective personalities, that their aspirations can almost be said to coincide with their self-definitions. Each of them has a uniquely personal conviction of who she is and of her inherent value as a human person. Despite the great differences in their external circumstances, the most basic aspiration of Elizabeth and Jane is to realize their own self-definitions by living according to the implications of their sense of self and by compelling their societies to acknowledge the validity of their self-definitions.

This is not to say that Elizabeth and Jane Eyre, or indeed any other two heroines, have precisely the same kinds of aspirations. Some aspirations, which are concrete and personal, depend upon the convergence of different factors: the heroine's family, her education, her social world, etc. The "concrete" ambitions are the kind which do admit of classification and categorization. Jane Eyre, for example, may be considered to have greater affinities with Maggie Tulliver than with Elizabeth Bennet, since both Jane and Maggie aspire to affection during lonely childhoods. Similarly, Elizabeth may seem closer to Emma than to Jane Eyre, since both Austen heroines inhabit social worlds where the chief interest is in marrying and giving in marriage.

The real likeness between Elizabeth Bennet and Jane Eyre does not derive from concrete, particularized aspirations. Rather, Jane and Elizabeth are most alike in their clear realization of their primary and fundamental need for the freedom to fulfill their personal sense of being. Both heroines, to different degrees, aspire to escape the "reality"--within and without--which would "reject and exclude" the fulfillment of their aspirations to personal freedom.

ELIZABETH BENNET

Elizabeth's most basic aspiration, for herself and for others, is happiness. A concordance to *Pride and Prejudice* would surely demonstrate that the word "happiness" is one of the terms most frequently employed by Elizabeth. Happiness, for Elizabeth, consists in the ability to act freely, to make independent personal choices, and to realize her sense of self-definition. For Elizabeth and Jane Austen, happiness is a highly normative term which means not the pursuit of pleasure and gratification but the pursuit of those pleasures which are suitable for rational beings. As defined by Elizabeth's society, happiness for a young lady consists in making a "good marriage." That is, a marriage which is materially beneficial and socially advantageous without regard to the personal affections of either party. Elizabeth's values and those of her society are in a complete deadlock. This conflict is illustrated through the way in which Elizabeth's view of certain marital matches departs from the conventional opinions of her society.

Elizabeth's society approves of Charlotte Lucas's pragmatic marriage to Mr. Collins "solely from the pure and disinterested desire of an establishment." (*P & P*, 93) Charlotte views her marriage with a sense of satisfaction:

> *Mr. Collins to be sure was neither sensible nor agreeable; his society was irksome, and his attachment to her must be imaginary. But still he would be her husband.--Without thinking highly either of men or of matrimony, marriage had always been her object; it was the only honourable provision for well-educated young women of small fortune, and however uncertain of giving happiness, must be their pleasantest preservative from want.* (P & P, 93)

To Charlotte, happiness in marriage is incidental. To Elizabeth, it is primary and basic. Her outward reaction to the news of Charlotte's engagement is highly ambivalent. Elizabeth wishes Charlotte "all imaginable happiness" (*P & P*, 95) but privately regrets that "it was impossible for that friend to be tolerably happy in the lot she had chosen." (*P & P*, 96)

Charlotte Lucas and Elizabeth become alienated because Elizabeth can no longer identify with her friend. Elizabeth feels that Charlotte has sacrificed that precious personal freedom to pursue true happiness which Elizabeth values so highly. While Charlotte defers to social convention from economic motives, Elizabeth's sister, Lydia, marries upon the basis of mere sexual attraction. Mrs. Bennet expresses the values of her society as she mindlessly rejoices at the news of Lydia's impending marriage:

> *"My dear, dear Lydia!" she [Mrs. Bennet] cried: "This is delightful indeed!--She will be married!--I shall see her again!--She will be married at sixteen! . . . But the clothes, the wedding clothes! I will write to my sister Gardiner about them directly. Lizzy, my dear, run down to your father and ask how much he will give her."* (P & P, 227)

In her secular, totally a-moral view of Lydia's imprudent marriage and in her concern with the externals of clothing and money, Mrs. Bennet epitomizes the commercial values of her society. While Mrs. Bennet's view is external and status-bound, Elizabeth's is primarily internal and personal. Elizabeth considers the marriage from a moral and emotional standpoint. It is a match which she cannot condone, because happiness has been sacrificed to sensuality and pragmatism. Elizabeth privately concludes that "rational happiness" cannot be expected for Lydia. (*P & P*, 228) She laments openly to Jane:

> *"How strange this is! And for this we are to be thankful. That they should marry, small as is their chance of happiness, and wretched as is his [Wickham's] character, we are forced to rejoice!* (P & P, 226)

Elizabeth is really an idealist who is trapped in a commercial, pragmatic society. She lyrically describes love as a "pure and elevating passion" (*P & P*, 114) and she approves of the marriage of Jane and Bingley not--as Mrs. Bennet does-- because Bingley "has four or five thousand a year, and very likely more" (*P & P*, 260) but rather, because the love of Jane and Bingley fulfills all of Elizabeth's ideal criteria for happiness in marriage: rationality, understanding, and a similarity of feelings and tastes:

116

> . . . *Elizabeth really believed all his [Bingley's] expectations*
> *of felicity, to be rationally founded, because they had for*
> *basis the excellent understanding, and super-excellent dis-*
> *position of Jane, and a general similarity of feeling and*
> *taste between her and himself.* (P & P, 259)

Elizabeth approves of the Jane-Bingley union mainly because this marriage, unlike Charlotte Lucas's or Lydia Bennet's, promises to extend the freedom of the parties involved. It is a marriage based upon love freely given and received and it involves two personalities which, by complementing one another, will be the means of each other's growth and ultimate fulfillment. This is the only kind of marriage which Elizabeth values and it is the kind of union which she desires for herself. In marrying Darcy, this particular aspiration of Elizabeth's is fulfilled, but only after she has first demonstrated the strength of her basic desire for individual freedom.

When Mr. Collins proposes to Elizabeth he provides her with the first real test of her aspiration to personal happiness and she is forced, for the first time, to articulate her commitment to the personal freedom to fulfill her definition of herself as a being of intrinsic value and worth. Mr. Collin's proposal to Elizabeth is predicated upon three basic stereotyped assumptions. Collins assumes that Elizabeth will be submissive to the claims of her society's hierarchy. He strongly implies that, in refusing him, Elizabeth will risk offending the sensitivities of Lady Catherine de Bourgh who has advised Mr. Collins to choose a wife who has "not [been] brought up high, but able to make a small income go a good way." (P & P, 80) Mr. Collins further assumes that since marriage is a pragmatic need of his, Elizabeth will consent to be the commodity which will fulfill this need. Finally, Mr. Collins operates upon the assumption that reciprocal love is in no way related to what he calls the "business" of marriage. His explanation of his own motivations in proposing to Elizabeth demonstrates the degree to which marriage is, to him, merely a necessary expedient:

> "*My reasons for marrying are, first that I think it a right*
> *thing for every clergyman in easy circumstances (like myself)*
> *to set the example of matrimony in his parish. Secondly,*
> *that I am convinced it will add very greatly to my happiness;*
> *and thirdly . . . that it is the particular advice and recom-*
> *mendation of the very noble lady whom I have the honour*
> *of calling patroness.*" (P & P, 80)

117

When Elizabeth refuses Mr. Collins, she opposes his commercial values to her own personal moral values by stating her commitment to personal happiness above social or economic conditions:

> "I do assure you that I am not one of those young ladies
> (if such young ladies there are) who are so daring as to risk
> their happiness on the chance of being asked a second time.
> I am perfectly serious in my refusal.--You could not make
> me happy, and I am convinced that I am the last woman in
> the world who would make you so." (P & P, 81)

It may at first appear that Elizabeth's rejection of Mr. Collins is a rather unspectacular demonstration of her aspiration to happiness since Mr. Collins, in his cold pride and obsequiousness, would seem to be a man whom any girl of sense would judge to be unacceptable. But the significance of Elizabeth's action is increased when Charlotte Lucas, who is Elizabeth's closest equal in intellect and wit, makes the very choice which Elizabeth so vehemently rejects. Actually, the strength of Elizabeth's commitment to her aspiration is best illustrated by examining a series of rejections and doubts: her rejection of Mr. Collins, her rejection of Darcy's first proposal, and her sincere doubts about the wisdom of accepting Darcy even after she realizes that she and Darcy entertain a mutual love for one another. Each rejection increases Elizabeth's isolation from her society's materialistic values and serves to sharpen the unique character of her aspiration and to demonstrate how, to Elizabeth, happiness and personal freedom are mutually dependent.

Elizabeth's rejection of the irritating Mr. Collins is perhaps a relatively easy choice for her in terms of moral sensitivity but a most difficult decision in terms of self-definition. Mr. Collins' offer of marriage forces Elizabeth publicly to assume a stance which, heretofore, had been a private conviction. In asserting the primacy of happiness over comfort, wealth and social position, Elizabeth declares her alienation from her society's values and renders herself vulnerable to the scrutiny and criticism of that society. Mr. Collins and Mrs. Bennet are effective spokespersons for their society's values and each feels free to insult and reproach Elizabeth because of her unconventional decision. Collins haughtily reminds Elizabeth that she is unlikely to receive another offer of marriage, while Mrs. Bennet upbraids Elizabeth for her lack of concern for the family's finances:

> *"But I tell you what, Miss Lizzy, if you take it into your head to go on refusing every offer of marriage in this way, you will never get a husband at all--and I am sure I do not know who is to maintain you when your father is dead.--I shall not be able to keep you--and so I warn you.--I have done with you from this day." (P & P, 86)*

The pressures which Mr. Collins and Mrs. Bennet, as typical members of society bring to bear upon Elizabeth represent external limitations to her aspiration. Indeed, society's demands force Elizabeth to assume the stance of a social heretic. Zea Zinn has noted how a girl's refusing to marry a man whom she despised "must have been a kind of heresy in the day when right-thinking parents considered family and property the basic grounds for marriage, and pooh-poohed what they called the romantic notions of their daughters who wanted to be able to respect if not love the men they married."[3] Although Elizabeth's materialistic society frustrates and complicates her quest for happiness, Elizabeth cannot fairly be considered a victim of her society. The limitations which Elizabeth's society imposes upon her serve only to increase the significance of her choices and decisions. Stuart Tave has remarked, "As boundaries become clear and close and alternatives are few and final, choice becomes more heroic."[4]

Elizabeth's irrational prejudice towards Darcy is an internal limitation to her aspiration which is equally as forceful as the external limitations which social codes and values present. Elizabeth's faulty image of herself as the omniscient perceiver, her tendency to make facile judgments and her sometimes irresponsible delight in her own wit constitute moral flaws which threaten to alienate her forever from the one person who is capable of helping her to fulfill her aspirations. Darcy's initial proposal to Elizabeth represents a severer test of her aspirations than did Mr. Collins' offer. Elizabeth's blind prejudice towards Darcy renders him disagreeable to her and functions to affect her reaction to him in a negative way which is somewhat equivalent to the negative effects of Mr. Collins' arrogant stupidity. Nonetheless, Darcy, as an intelligent gentleman, holds an appeal for Elizabeth which Mr. Collins did not:

> *"In spite of her [Elizabeth's] deeply-rooted dislike [of Darcy], she could not be insensible to the compliment of such a man's affection, and though her intentions did not vary for an instant, she was at first sorry for the pain he was to receive." (P & P, 142)*

Elizabeth is attracted to Darcy despite her prejudice and this is clearly demonstrated when her reasons for refusing him are examined. She resents his essentially correct estimate of her family connections but, even more, Elizabeth resents what she deems to have been Darcy's interference with the happiness of Jane, Bingley and Mr. Wickham. Elizabeth does not refuse Darcy on purely personal grounds; nowhere does she assert that he has interfered with her own potential for happiness. Essentially, Elizabeth is forced to refuse Darcy purely on the strength of her belief in the principle of happiness with little of the external motivation which Mr. Collins' obnoxiousness afforded in that earlier proposal scene. Mr. Collins had predicted that Elizabeth would be unlikely to receive another offer of marriage. When Elizabeth does receive Darcy's unexpected proposal and then rejects him, the strength of her aspiration is striking. As Elizabeth's options narrow, the intensity of her aspiration only increases. Unlike Charlotte Lucas or Mr. Bingley, Elizabeth cannot be panicked into settling for anything less than what, to her, is the very best.

The most telling test of Elizabeth's aspiration occurs after she has shed her illusory self-image and has become aware of the true nature of Darcy's character. Darcy's conduct upon the occasion of her visit to Pemberley and his subsequent attentions convince Elizabeth that there is a mutual undeclared love between herself and Darcy. The Pemberley estate is, in a certain sense, an image of Elizabeth's aspiration to happiness and freedom. The estate is well-ordered but natural and it exhibits grace without denying the freedom of nature:

> It [Pemberley House] was a large, handsome, stone building, standing well on rising ground, and backed by a ridge of high woody hills;--and in front, a stream of some natural importance was swelled into greater, but without any artificial appearance. Its banks were neither formal nor falsely adorned. (P & P, 181)

Pemberley House delights Elizabeth because it symbolically demonstrates that freedom and social order are not necessarily mutually exclusive. She sees in the estate an affirmation of her desire for freedom which leads to a personal realization that happiness and self-fulfillment might be possible for the mistress of Pemberley.

Elizabeth intuitively realizes that she might fulfill her fundamental desire for freedom and her personal aspiration for happiness as mistress of Pemberley. Still, Elizabeth hesitates to reveal her true feelings to Darcy himself. Her hesitation is an illustration of the ultimate sincerity of her aspiration, for she is not now confronted with making a decision about an unacceptable man, as was the case with Mr. Collins, nor is she blinded by prejudice or subject to societal pressures. Rather, Elizabeth hesitates out of a pure concern for the mutual happiness of Darcy and of herself.

> *She respected, she esteemed, she was grateful to him [Darcy], she felt a real interest in his welfare; and she only wanted to know how far she wished that welfare to depend upon herself, and how far it would be for the happiness of both that she should employ the power, which her fancy told her she still possessed, of bringing on the renewal of his addresses.* (P & P, 197)

Like Jane Eyre, who is forced to make decisions solely upon the strength of religious principles, Elizabeth must make a desicion which is based upon her principle of happiness as the highest good. Only when she is certain that her aspirations to personal freedom and happiness will be fulfilled does Elizabeth consent to marry Darcy. Elizabeth's marriage assures her the freedom she had sought so strenuously to maintain. In Darcy she has found a partner who respects her definition of herself as a unique person with the potential for growth and happiness. The marriage which fulfills Elizabeth's aspirations may seem to be a rather undramatic kind of freedom for an aspiring, talented heroine. But, in Jane Austen's vision, the best love provides the truest kind of personal freedom, for love demands the appreciation of the beloved as different and unique. In a very real sense, Elizabeth's marriage is not an ordinary "happy ending" but a radical fulfillment: it signifies the deeply-rooted need of every human being to realize the peculiarly human ontological sense of being.

Like Elizabeth Bennet, Jane Eyre struggles to attain the freedom which will permit her to realize her own self-definition and also like Elizabeth, Jane's desire for this freedom is conscious and relatively uncomplicated. While the basic human desire for individual freedom underlies the aspirations of all five talented heroines, Jane Eyre and Elizabeth Bennet stand apart in that they, of all the heroines, are most acutely conscious of the way in which a sense of personal freedom is an absolute prerequisite to the fulfillment of more precise and personal aspirations such as aspirations to love, knowledge, social status, etc. Jane and Elizabeth possess this clarity of vision and are able singlemindedly to struggle for personal freedom because each of them is sustained by a strong and adequate self-definition. Elizabeth, as we have seen, defines herself almost in terms of existential loneliness. She realizes that she alone can create herself as a complete and unique person. Elizabeth further realizes that she must assert the reality of her unique being as a person in the face of a society which conspires to reduce her to the status of a commodity. Despite her great moral sensitivity, Elizabeth is part of a society which is presented as operating in an essentially secular and materialistic way. Hence, her aspiration for freedom can only be articulated and realized in secular terms. Jane Eyre, by contrast, is really a member of no one society and her self-definition stems from her own inward religious vision. The self-definition which she strives to realize is her sense of herself as a free child of God.

JANE EYRE

Few will deny that *Jane Eyre* is a novel which is concerned with freedom. But what sort of freedom? In 1848 Lady Eastlake condemned the novel as an anti-Christian document which encouraged social rebellion:

> *Altogether the auto-biography of* Jane Eyre *is pre-eminently an anti-Christian composition. There is throughout it a murmuring against the comforts of the rich and against the privations of the poor, which, as far as each individual is concerned, is a murmuring against God's appointment--there is a proud and perpetual assertion of the rights of man, for which we find no authority either in God's word or in God's providence--there is that pervading tone of ungodly discontent which is at once the most prominent and the most subtle evil which the law and the pulpit, which all civilized society in fact has at the present day to contend with. We do not hesitate to say that the tone of mind and thought which has overthrown authority and violated every code human and divine abroad, and fostered Chartism and rebellion at home, is the same which has also written* Jane Eyre.[5]

A modern critic has described *Jane Eyre* as "a feminist tract, an argument for the social betterment of governesses and equal rights for women."[6] Another recent critic has demurred:

The novel [Jane Eyre] is frequently cited as the earliest major feminist novel, although there is not a hint in the book of any desire for political, legal, educational, or even intellectual equality between the sexes. Miss Bronte asks only the simple--or is it the most complex?--recognition that the same heart and the same spirit animate both men and women, and that love is the pairing of equals in these spheres.[7]

Apart from the usual tendency of critics to disagree, these differing interpretations can perhaps be explained by recognizing that *Jane Eyre* is a novel about various kinds of freedom and different levels of freedom and that Jane herself entertains multiple aspirations which differ in intensity and depth. On a basic level, *Jane Eyre* is the story of a heroine who is constantly confronted with various threats to her physical, moral and psychological freedom. The novel begins with Jane's physical imprisonment in the red room at Gateshead Hall. At Lowood Jane suffers a psychological incarceration which makes her gasp for liberty and pray for a "new servitude." Her "new servitude" brings her to Thornfield where her love for Mr. Rochester threatens her moral freedom. Jane escapes moral imprisonment only to be confronted with the psychic imprisonment which the zeal of St. John Rivers constitutes for her. Jane triumphs over all of these obstacles and, of course, is ultimately rewarded through attaining union with the man whom she loves.

One way of viewing *Jane Eyre*, then, is to see Jane's story as a progressive series of negations--Jane's ultimate triumph is possible because she has succeeded in denying or in defeating those persons and situations which threaten her freedom and integrity. On another level, however, it is also possible to view Jane's story as a process of affirmation. Jane defines herself as the beloved child of a providential God and this self-definition confers upon her a basic freedom which the Mrs. Reeds and St. John Rivers of the world cannot take away. Hence, however inhibiting her external circumstances may be, Jane views herself as an inherently free being whose task is to be faithful to her self-definition. Each obstacle or negation provides Jane with another opportunity to affirm her freedom and to fulfill the destiny which she feels providence has arranged for her. We can, then, talk about at least two levels of freedom in *Jane Eyre*. One kind of freedom is the condition of being free from external restrictions and is essentially a negative sort of freedom because its essence is the absence of restraint. It is this sort of freedom for which Jane longs when she expresses her dissatisfaction with her monotonous existence as a governess:

> *Women are supposed to be very calm generally: but women feel just as men feel; they need exercise for their faculties and a field for their efforts as much as their brothers do; they suffer from too rigid a restraint, too absolute a stagnation, precisely as men would suffer; and it is narrow-minded in their more privileged fellow-creatures to say that they ought to confine themselves to making puddings and knitting stockings, to playing on the piano and embroidering bags. It is thoughtless to condemn them, or laugh at them, if they seek to do more or learn more than custom has pronounced necessary for their sex.* (JE, 96)

The second level of freedom which operates in *Jane Eyre* is of a more positive nature and consists of Jane's conviction that, by virtue of her existence as a child of God, she possesses an interior liberty of spirit. It is the sense of this freedom which enables Jane to assert her equality "before God" with Mr. Rochester and to declare, "I am no bird; and no net ensnares me: I am a free human being with an independent will; which I now exert to leave you." *(JE, 223)*

Just as there are two levels of freedom in *Jane Eyre* so, too, one may discern two levels of aspiration. The most basic level consists of various concrete aspirations of Jane's which differ in intensity and importance. These aspirations range from a superficial desire for physical beauty *(JE, 86)*, to a desire for independence which makes Jane insist upon working even after her projected marriage. She tells Rochester: "I will not be your English Celine Varens. I shall continue to act as Adele's governess; by that I shall earn my board and lodging, and thirty pounds a year besides. I'll furnish my own wardrobe out of that money." *(JE, 237)* The most intense of Jane's concrete aspirations is, of course, her aspiration to the love of Mr. Rochester. So intense is her aspiration to Rochester's love that it interferes with Jane's broader spiritual aspiration to find her destiny by fulfilling her definition of herself as a child of God. Jane herself realizes that these two levels of aspiration conflict, although she does not at the time realize the true nature of the threat to her self-definition which this conflict will generate:

> *My future husband was becoming to me my whole world;*

124

*and more than the world: almost my hope of heaven. He
stood between me and every thought of religion, as an
eclipse intervenes between man and the broad sun. I could
not, in those days, see God for his creature: of whom I had
made an idol.* (JE, 241)

Jane's aspiration to fulfill her self-definition as a child of God does ultimately
triumph over her concrete aspiration to Rochester's love. In "planting her
foot" upon the rock of God's laws Jane asserts the primacy of her spiritual
aspirations over even the most intensely concrete aspiration.

Jane's various personal and concrete aspirations are often facets of her desire
freely to work out her providential destiny. Just as the Pemberley estate
functions as an image of Elizabeth Bennet's aspirations to happiness and freedom, certain religious images and motifs operate in *Jane Eyre* to illuminate the
nature of Jane's aspirations. The religious imagery functions both to reveal
Jane's providential vision and to demonstrate how Jane's actions and decisions are motivated by her aspiration to fulfill her self-definition.

When Jane leaves Thornfield after refusing to live as Rochester's mistress, she
implicitly invites a comparison of herself with Lot's wife: "No reflection was
to be allowed now: not one glance was to be cast back; not even one forward."
(*JE*, 282) As she progresses on her journey from Thornfield, Jane is overcome
by hunger. Like the prodigal son, she longs for the waste which she sees being
fed to swine: "At the door of a cottage I saw a little girl about to throw a mess
of cold porridge into a pig trough. 'Will you give me that?' I asked." (*JE*, 290)
Both of these Biblical allusions demonstrate how Jane's vision of life is essentially a providential one. The allusion to Lot's wife indicates her awareness of
God's justice and her conviction that, in leaving Rochester, she had followed
the guidance of providence and must not weaken in her endeavor. The allusion
to the prodigal son demonstrates Jane's concept of God's mercy and the vision
of life as a kind of moral pilgrimage which ends in the embrace of a loving
father.

Religious imagery is often invoked to indicate Jane's awareness that she has
performed some act which is in harmony with her self-definition. Her flight
from Rochester was one such act which affirmed her freedom to fulfill her
spiritual destiny. When Jane finally reaches the haven of the Rivers' home, she
notes that she slept for three days and three nights. The implicit allusion to

the Resurrection suggests that Jane has abandoned an old life and is about to begin a new phase of her destiny at the Rivers' home.

Perhaps the most effective use of religious imagery occurs when Eucharistic images are employed to illustrate Jane's aspiration to be loved. As a frightened and lonely child at Lowood, Jane finds solace and comfort in the love feast which Miss Temple provides:

> *Having invited Helen and me to approach the table, and placed before each of us a cup of tea with one delicious but thin morsel of toast, she [Miss Temple] got up, unlocked a drawer, and taking from it a parcel wrapped in paper, disclosed presently to our eyes a good-sized seedcake.* (JE, 63)

When, exhausted and homeless, Jane arrives at the Rivers home, Diana Rivers offers love to Jane through a symbolic communion:

> *Diana . . . broke some bread, dipped it in milk, and put it to my lips. Her face was near mine: I saw there was pity in it, and I felt sympathy in her hurried breathing. In her simple words, too, the same balm-like emotion spoke: "Try to eat."* (JE, 296)

When, through the intervention of providence, Jane is reunited with Rochester at Ferndean, she is not the recipient of love but rather the minister of their symbolic communion. Jane approaches Rochester with candles and water which suggest the new light she will bring to his life and the refreshed spirit which her love will provide. At this moment Jane has attained the fulfillment of the self-definition to which she had aspired. Mr. Rochester recognizes both her humanity and her freedom. She is no longer an "elf," "fairy" or "sprite" to him but "altogether a human being." (JE, 385) Rochester no longer sees Jane as a stereotyped angel to adorn and transform. He is anxious for their wedding, and contemptuously dismisses the finery which he had once insisted upon: "Never mind fine clothes and jewels now: all that is not worth a fillup." (JE, 393)

Jane attains her ultimate happiness because she has been faithful to her aspiration to fulfill her destiny as a free child of God. Her reward for being true to herself is a union in which her former aspiration to Rochester's love is reconciled with her desire to fulfill her specific providential destiny. Jane can apply

126

the words of the Virgin Mary to herself--"I kept these things then, and pondered them in my heart" (JE, 394)--because her own happiness, like Mary's, has proved to be synonymous with her providential destiny.

The external limitations which appear to threaten Jane Eyre's freedom are relatively powerless against the internal sense of freedom which her own self-definition affords. The only real internal threat to Jane's freedom occurs when she is tempted to abandon her self-definition and to forget God in making an idol of Mr. Rochester (JE, 241) The situation of another talented heroine, Emma Woodhouse, is as different from Jane Eyre's as could possibly be imagined. Unlike Jane, Emma's aspirations are threatened by a host of internal, as well as external, limitations. Lacking the honest and appropriate sense of self-definition which sustains Elizabeth Bennet and Jane Eyre, Emma's quest for personal freedom is additionally complicated by the fact that she has no conscious knowledge of her subconscious desire for personal freedom. Emma knows that she wants to create, but she does not realize that her first obligation is freely and responsibly to create herself by fully realizing her human potential.

EMMA WOODHOUSE

Emma's aspirations can only be fully understood against the background of the limitations--both external and internal--which threaten them. If we are to appreciate Emma as more than a meanly manipulative aspirant to power, we must first understand the limitations of Emma's social world.

The world of Highbury society is one in which the commonplace prevails and in which singularity is suspect. The intellectual mediocrity of Emma's society is well characterized by Jane Austen's description of the quality of the conversation at the Cole's dinner party:

> The rest of the dinner passed away; the dessert succeeded,
> the children came in, and were talked to and admired amid
> the usual rate of conversation; a few clever things said, a
> few downright silly, but by much the larger proportion
> neither the one nor the other--nothing worse than every day
> remarks, dull repetitions, old news, and heavy jokes. (E, 148)

A static parochialism contributes to the overwhelmingly mediocre ambience of

Highbury. After Emma realizes her error in having intended Harriet for Mr. Elton, her confined social world provides an additional source of suffering:

> *Their [Emma, Harriet, Mr. Elton] being fixed, so absolutely fixed, in the same place, was bad for each, for all three. Not one of them had the power of removal, or of effecting any material change of society. They must encounter each other, and make the best of it. (E, 97)*

The limitations of Emma's society often vex and frustrate her. But, like Elizabeth Bennet, she is able to employ her intellectual acuity and to view her claustrophobic world with detached amusement. While Harriet lingers over the dry goods in Ford's shop, Emma walks to the door "for amusement." The mundane details which constitute life in Highbury are related as they are perceived by Emma's acute intelligence:

> *Much could not be hoped for the traffic of even the busiest part of Highbury;--Mr. Perry walking hastily by, Mr. William Cox letting himself in at the office door, Mr. Cole's carriage horses returning from exercise, or a stray letter-boy or an obstinate mule, were the liveliest objects she could presume to expect; and when her eyes fell only on the butcher with his tray, a tidy old woman travelling homewards from shop with her full basket, two curs quarrelling over a dirty bone, and a string of dawdling children round the baker's bow-window eyeing the gingerbread, she knew she had no reason to complain, and was amused enough; quite enough still to stand at the door. A mind lively and at ease, can do with seeing nothing, and can see nothing that does not answer. (E, 157-158)*

Highbury life is presented as an accumulation of petty, banal, even sordid minutiae. The related details overwhelm the reader with a sense of the inhibiting, prosaic and unimaginative conditions which characterize Emma's world. But Emma herself is neither oppressed nor disgusted. Her acute imaginative sense enables her to transform a rather depressing spectacle into a scene which she can view with wry detachment. Emma's lively imagination constitutes her salvation from Highbury's mediocrity and also presents one of the severest limitations to her own self-fulfillment.

Emma Woodhouse dominates Highbury society by virtue of her social, external status. But, while she is in her society, Emma is not of it. Her wit, intelligence and imagination distinguish her from a society which values conformity and mediocrity. Early in the novel, Emma is presented as unique by virtue of her intelligence. With the departure of Miss Weston, Emma is in "great danger of suffering from intellectual solitude" for the village of Highbury "afforded her no equals." (E, 2) Mr. Knightley is aware of Emma's isolation from her society and of the possible dangers which her singularity of wit and intellect may occasion. He expresses his apprehension to Mrs. Weston:

> "She [Emma] always declares she will never marry . . . But I have no idea that she has yet ever seen a man she cared for. It would not be a bad thing for her to be very much in love, with a proper object. I should like to see Emma in love, and in some doubt of a return; it would do her good. But there is nobody hereabouts to attach her; and she goes so seldom from home." (E, 26)

Emma's innate intelligence is accompanied by a keen but unrefined imaginative sense. Emma is instinctively creative and her undisciplined imagination enables her to cope with the tedium of Highbury life by transforming ordinary events into romantic fictions and mysteries. Emma's imaginative creativity is a conscious expression of her unconscious need to create herself by fulfilling the unrealized potential to which her intelligence, wit and imagination attest. Emma is unaware of her need for the personal freedom to create herself chiefly because she is trapped by the limitations of a dishonest self-definition: she mistakenly identifies the freedom to manipulate with the ontological freedom of being. This error leads Emma to exhibit a conventional self-definition in order to operate and dominate more "freely" in her society.

It has often been remarked by critics that Emma's real aspiration is to dominate and control. There is no doubt that the desire for power motivates Emma; we have seen how this aspiration leads to an illusory self-image and to an essentially dishonest self-definition. To say that Emma aspires to power is, however, rather like saying that Jane Eyre aspires to win Mr. Rochester's hand. Both statements are true, but both are simplistic and fail to do justice to the complexity of the heroines' characters and aspirations. A closer examination of Emma's aspirations reveals that her compulsion to create fictions is an analogue of the human desire to fulfill oneself. The limitations which threaten Emma's creativity warp her aspiration to create and allow it to find only a perverted expression through her apparent aspiration to power.

Emma employs her imaginative creativity as a defense against the mediocrity which characterizes her society and which she fears will overwhelm her. Her initial plan to match Harriet Smith and Mr. Elton is characterized less by a blatant desire for power than by a wish to assert her personal uniqueness by demonstrating the originality of her mind:

> *Mr. Elton was the very person fixed on by Emma for driving the young farmer out of Harriet's head. She thought it would be an excellent match; and only too palpably desirable, natural, and probable, for her to have much merit in planning it. She feared it was what every body else must think of and predict. (E, 21-22)*

Emma's desire to distinguish herself through imaginative creativity has most often been censured as socially disruptive, as in the instances of the Harriet-Elton, Frank Churchill-Harriet, and Jane Fairfax-Mr. Dixon matches. The moral irresponsibility of Emma's actions has often deflected attention from the creative fictional talent which these imaginary matches display. It is seldom recognized that Emma's creativity is as often employed in harmless reverie as in social manipulation and interference. For example, Emma's imaginary description of Frank Churchill, before she has met him, reveals a latent talent for fictional characterization:

> *"My idea of him [Frank] is, that he can adapt his conversation to the taste of every body, and, has the power as well as the wish of being universally agreeable. To you, he will talk of farming; to me, of drawing or music; and so on to every body, having that general information on all subjects which will enable him to follow the lead, or take the lead, just as propriety may require, and to speak extremely well on each; that is my idea of him." (E, 102)*

Emma's painting of Harriet also reveals her predilection for creativity, as does her fondness for puzzles, charades, and word-games.

Just as Pemberley in *Pride and Prejudice* and religious imagery in *Jane Eyre* serve to illustrate the nature of the heroines' aspirations, so too, the use of games and puzzles in *Emma* points to Emma's aspiration to create as well as to the limitations to her aspirations. Highbury society is basically indifferent to talent, singularity, or to a delight in intellectual exercise for its own sake. Emma enjoys the wit displayed in Mr. Elton's charade, only to find that Harriet is too dense to share in her delight. (*E*, 48) Frank Churchill engages Emma's intellect by beginning a word game, but it soon becomes obvious that this is a mere stratagem for gaining the attention of Jane Fairfax. (*E*, 283) The languor and disapproval with which the Box Hill party receives Emma's lively attempt at conundrums is symptomatic of her society's indifference to that which is different, challenging, or intellectually stimulating.

The philistinism of Highbury society presents external limitations to Emma's desire to distinguish herself by creative display. Even more powerful, however, are the internal limitations which Emma's own nature provides. It is true that part of the reason why Emma turns to the manipulation of others is that her society provides no constructive outlet for her imaginative energies. But it is also true that Emma does little to refine and channel her imagination. Emma lacks the self-discipline needed for true creativity and her imagination is unchecked by her reason. Mr. Knightly observes: "But I have done with expecting any course of steady reading from Emma. She will never submit to any thing requiring industry and patience, and a subjection of the fancy to the understanding." (*E*, 23) The result of Emma's creative desire to paint illustrates the truth of Mr. Knightley's remark. Emma has made "many beginnings" but has never completed a portrait:

> *She had always wanted to do everything, and had made more progress both in drawing and music than many might have done with so little labour as she would ever submit to. She played and sang;--and drew in almost every style; but steadiness had always been wanting; and in nothing had she approached the degree of excellence which she would have been glad to command, and ought not to have failed of.*
> (E, 28)

Emma is a perfectionist and she exhibits all of the perfectionist's perverse pride. Her social world is repellent to her and offers her no constructive channel for her talents. On the other hand, Emma's pride and irresolution prevent her from committing herself wholeheartedly to any work, for fear of the vulnerability which failure might bring. Her own limitations and the pressures

131

of her society ultimately lead Emma to a perverted exercise of her imaginative powers. Highbury society is not fond of discussing ideas, but it delights in gossiping about people. In pandering to her society's parochialism and her own pride of imagination, Emma distorts her creative desires. Only self-knowledge can make Emma see that imagination can be employed destructively as well as constructively. When Emma marries Mr. Knightley she is rather like an unfinished painting. We are left to assume that Knightley's respect for her talents and his steady reliability will complement Emma as she strives to fulfill her human potential and to complete her own self-portrait.

While Emma becomes belatedly conscious of the need for personal freedom which so strongly motivates Elizabeth Bennet and Jane Eyre, George Eliot's heroines seem to fear the responsibility which accompanies personal freedom. Dorothea Brooke and Maggie Tulliver both possess various large-scale, heroic aspirations and unrelated theoretic ideals. Both heroines feel intellectually and emotionally frustrated by their inability to reconcile their aspirations with their theoretic preconceptions. The burden of intellectual freedom is temporarily removed when each heroine finds an illusory kind of control which, she believes, will make her life meaningful and her suffering bearable. While the stories of Elizabeth Bennet and Jane Eyre demonstrate how desirable freedom can be to the talented heroine, the stories of Dorothea Brooke and Maggie Tulliver illustrate how anxiety can threaten the talented heroine as she strives for the freedom to realize her aspirations.

DOROTHEA BROOKE

The young Dorothea Brooke enjoys a considerable amount of intellectual freedom. Although she is handicapped by a "narrow and promiscuous" education, Dorothea possesses the intellectual vigor to pursue learning independently. When the novel begins, Dorothea is depicted as possessing a number of concrete ambitions which coexist uneasily in her mind with a mass of heroic ideals. Dorothea's concrete ambitions include her social interests in an infant school, in cottage building and aspirations to acquire knowledge. Her heroic ideals, although unarticulated, include a vague general desire for "some lofty conception of the world which might frankly include the parish of Tipton and her own rule of conduct there." (M, 6) Dorothea seems to associate this "lofty conception" with various forms of self-denial, including fasting, reading late into the night, praying on the stone floor beside sick laborers and renouncing the pleasures of beautiful jewels. Dorothea acquires her theory from Pascal and Jeremy Taylor; her dilemma consists in an inability to relate theoretic conception to real life:

> Dorothea knew many passages of Pascal's Pensees and of Jeremy Taylor by heart; and to her the destinies of mankind, seen by the light of Christianity, made the solicitudes of feminine fashion appear an occupation for Bedlam. She could not renconcile the anxieties of a spiritual life involving eternal consequences, with a keen interest in guimp and artificial protrusions of drapery. (M, 6)

Dorothea is frustrated because her many individual acts of self-denial fail to yield the comprehensive world view for which she yearns. Dorothea wants to be learned and she wants to be pious; in her youthful enthusiasm she identifies the two and encounters only frustration when she fails to synthesize knowledge, piety, and everyday life in the Parish of Tipton. She exhibits all the symptoms of an overwrought, anxiety-ridden mind in her reply to Celia's request that they examine their mother's jewels:

> "Of course, then, let us have them [the jewels] out. Why did you not tell me before? But the keys, the keys!" She pressed her hands against the sides of her head and seemed to despair of her memory. (M, 9)

Dorothea is truly in search of "the keys." Her intellectual frustrations have convinced her that her disjointed world view is a product of her own ignorance and that there exists a sort of magic formula which will synthesize her concrete attempts at piety and knowledge with her desire for a lofty conception of the world. Dorothea has used her freedom to pursue ideas which she is intellectually and emotionally unequipped to handle. She lacks the ability to synthesize disparate bits of information as well as the patience or negative capability to dwell in an area of intellectual incertitude. Dorothea is concerned about her own salvation and unable to tolerate the anxiety which her intellectual freedom produces. It is not surprising that she looks to the author of the "Key to All Mythologies" to provide a key to her own dilemma and to impose a measure of control upon her fragmented intellectual life.

Dorothea's engagement to Mr. Casaubon represents a new phase in the evolution of her aspirations. She puts aside, although she does not forget, her former concrete ambitions—such as her plans for cottages. She resolves to devote herself first to learning the "completest knowledge" from Mr. Casaubon and she willingly exchanges her intellectual freedom for Mr. Casaubon's "wise" control:

> *The union which attracted her was one that would deliver her from her girlish subjection to her own ignorance, and give her the freedom of voluntary submission to a guide who would take her along the grandest path. (M, 21)*

We have seen how Dorothea comes to realize that her husband is incapable of showing her the "grand path." Early in her marriage she suppresses her personal aspirations that she might learn from her husband. Later, Dorothea renounces her former aspirations out of a sense of wifely duty and servitude. Dorothea comes to long for that freedom of spirit which she had so trustingly and so naively offered to Mr. Casaubon:

> *This afternoon the helplessness was more wretchedly benumbing than ever: she longed for objects who could be dear to her, and to whom she could be dear. She longed for work which would be directly beneficent like the sunshine and the rain, and now it appeared that she was to live more and more in a virtual tomb, where there was the apparatus of a ghastly labour producing what would never see the light. (M, 348)*

During this final unhappy period of her marriage, Dorothea comes to realize that she had unconsciously aspired to more than the intellectual control and pious servitude of which she had been conscious. She had also aspired to love and companionship and the miniature of Will Ladislaw's grandmother acts as a kind of image of this aspiration. Will's grandmother, who risked all for love and chose to be vulnerable and free rather than safe and controlled, represents human values which Dorothea is slowly growing to appreciate.

After the death of Mr. Casaubon, Lydgate examines Dorothea and prescribes a remedy: "She wants perfect freedom, I think, more than any other prescription." (*M*, 360) The mature Dorothea is marked by a loss of her former heroic, theoretic ideals. She is able to cope with freedom, is open to others, willing to risk vulnerability and no longer anxious to be in a state of perfect control:

"In the long valley of her life, which looked so flat and empty of way marks, guidance would come as she walked along the road, and saw her fellow-passengers by the way." (*M*, 367)

The progression of Dorothea's sense of aspiration parallels the life of St. Theresa as it is described in the *Prelude*. As a young girl, Dorothea is as ardent, impetuous and impractical as the young Theresa who seeks martyrdom among the Moors. As a mature woman Dorothea resembles the saint in her cloister: her life is hidden to the world, but the effects of her being are "incalculably diffusive." The life lived for others, like comtemplative prayer, is unspectacular, and unheroic but powerfully beneficent. Dorothea does not live an ideal life, but in her goodness and openness to others she lives a life as close to Theresa's ideal as is possible in nineteenth century England.

Through her openness to others, Dorothea is able to help two other aspirers who, like herself, have fallen short of their original heroic ideals. In giving the Lowick living to Mr. Farebrother she provides him with the scope which he needs to renew his faith in himself as a cleric. In supporting Lydgate in the face of society's opposition, Dorothea makes it possible for him to remain in Middlemarch, although she cannot erase his sense of failure. Like Dorothea, Lydgate had once entertained heroic ambitions and, like her, he has failed to fulfill' them. Dorothea's inadequate education led her into an imprudent marriage, just as Lydgate's "spots of commonness" made him easy prey for Rosamund, his basil plant. Lydgate's failure seems the more concrete one: he possessed the intelligence, ability and zeal to revolutionize the practice of medicine in Middlemarch. While Dorothea maintains that "there was always something better which she might have done, if she had only been better and known better," (*M*, 610) it is difficult to imagine what this "something" might have been. Unlike those of Lydgate, Dorothea's heroic aspirations were never clearly articulated. Her early state of aspiration was really an emotionally-charged state of religious zeal without concrete or formalized goals.

Dorothea, considered only as an aspirer, may disappoint us. In marrying Will she gives up her claim to funds with which she might have done a great deal of social good. She never carries out her cottage scheme because "Sir James and my uncle have convinced me [Dorothea] that the risk would be too great." (*M*, 560) She marries someone who will work for good in a prosaic, unspectacular way, laboring among the inglorious maze of obscure parliamentary committees. Dorothea is not an example of heroic aspiration spectacularly fulfilled.

She is, however, an example of how the talented heroine can overcome social limitations and personal limitations in order to fulfill her potential as a woman and as a free human being.

MAGGIE TULLIVER

Elizabeth Bennet and Jane Eyre succeed in fulfilling their aspirations, while Emma gains the hand of the man she loves and adopts worthier aspirations. Only Dorothea Brooke and Maggie Tulliver exhibit a progression of aspirations which are never completely fulfilled. Like the young Dorothea and the young St. Theresa, the child Maggie exhibits large scale ambitions. When she runs away to the gypsy camp, she reminds one of Theresa toddling off to face the Moors. Like Dorothea, Maggie yearns for a number of unrelated ideals, including love, beauty, and knowledge. Maggie's aspirations are limited by her inferior education; she has received only a mixture of "smattering, extraneous information" (*MF*, 125) and her moral training has left her "quite without that knowledge of the irreversible laws within and without her, which, governing the habits, becomes morality, and, developing the feelings of submission and dependence, becomes religion." (*MF*, 252-253)

When Maggie is left alone and emotionally isolated after Mr. Tulliver's bankruptcy, the long, free, empty days leave her free to indulge in melancholy, bitter and resentful thoughts. She desires an explanation of "this hard real life" and, like the troubled Dorothea, Maggie imagines that knowledge will provide a panacea for her anxiety:

> *She wanted some key that would enable her to understand, and, in understanding, endure, the heavy weight that had fallen on her young heart. If she had been taught "real learning and wisdom, such as great men knew," she thought she should have held the secrets of life; if she had only books, that she might learn for herself what wise men knew!* (MF, 251)

Maggie looks to the doctrine of renunciation of *The Imitation of Christ* just as Dorothea once looked to Mr. Casaubon. Both heroines hope to introduce a measure of control and order into their confused lives. Maggie attempts to eliminate the pain of desiring love, learning, and beauty by banishing her aspiration for these things. She need not have chosen the way of renunciation:

136

Philip Wakem desires Maggie's friendship and wishes to share his love of books and music with her. But, in choosing renunciation Maggie adopts the only course which will not conflict with her self-definition. She explains her decision to Philip:

> "I've been a great deal happier," she [Maggie] said at last, timidly, "since I have given up thinking about what is easy and pleasant, and being discontented because I couldn't have my own will. Our life is determined for us--and it makes the mind very free when we give up wishing, and only think of bearing what is laid upon us, and doing what is given us to do." (MF, 264)

Like Dorothea, Maggie chooses not to be free in an effort to simplify her life and shield herself from painful choices. Maggie soon finds that superficial asceticism brings only a negative peace. Stephen Guest represents "a world of love and beauty and delight" and Maggie discovers that her renunciation had repressed but not eliminated her aspirations:

> It was not that she thought distinctly of Mr. Stephen Guest . . . ; it was rather that she felt the half-remote presence of a world of love and beauty and delight, made up of vague, mingled images from all the poetry and romance she had ever read, or had ever woven in her dreamy reveries. Her mind glanced back once or twice to the time when she had courted privation, when she had thought all longing, all impatience, was subdued; but that condition seemed irrevocably gone, and she recoiled from the remembrance of it. No prayer, no striving now, would bring back that negative peace: the battle of her life, it seemed, was not to be decided in that short and easy way--by perfect renunciation at the very threshold of her youth. The music was vibrating in her still. (MF, 335-336)

When Stephen Guest proposes marriage to Maggie, he offers her the freedom to fulfill all of her long-repressed aspirations. As Stephen's wife, she will receive the love she has craved and knowledge, beauty and music will be available to her. When Maggie rejects Stephen she seems to renounce her freedom. She does, indeed, give up all hope of a future which will include love and beauty.

But, by the act of renouncing her personal ambitions, Maggie affirms her fundamental human freedom to create herself through free moral choice:

> *"We can't choose happiness either for ourselves or for another: we can't tell where that will lie. We can only choose whether we will indulge ourselves in the present moment, or whether we will renounce that, for the sake of obeying the divine voice within us--for the sake of being true to all the motives that sanctify our lives." (MF, 419)*

Maggie achieves true freedom at this moment of choice and yet her decision is one that fails to satisfy the reader in the same way that Jane Eyre's rejection of Rochester does. In part, Maggie's choice seems less than satisfactory because "the motives that sanctify our lives" include a self-repressive definition of herself in terms of family ties and obligations. Chiefly, however, Maggie's dilemma is unsettling because of its complexity. In the cases of the other talented heroines, the basic desire for personal freedom ultimately harmonized with the heroines' particular, concrete aspirations. In Maggie's case this is not so. In choosing to assert her freedom to be her best self, Maggie renounces forever her personal aspirations to love, learning, music and beauty.

Like *Middlemarch*, *The Mill on the Floss* forces us to recognize the complexity of free choice. Ultimately, Eliot compels us to realize that the human condition precludes perfect fulfillment or perfect freedom. Maggie's unfulfilled aspirations are analogous to Dorothea's abandoned heroic ideals. As we consider Maggie's determining choice, we are reminded of Marcel's metaphor: creating oneself is a kind of birth and, as such, involves pain as well as potential fulfillment.

Chapter 6

CONCLUSION:
THE INTEGRATION OF SELF AND SOCIETY

To try and approach truth on one side after another, not to strive or cry, nor to persist in pressing forward, on any one side, with violence and self-will,--it is only thus, it seems to me, that mortals may hope to gain any vision of the mysterious Goddess, whom we shall never see except in outline, but only thus even in outline.[1]

In attempting to free the Victorians from what he deemed to be a dogmatic, insular temper of mind, Matthew Arnold urged English thinkers to adopt an attitude of "disinterestedness" and to allow "a free play of the mind on all subjects which it touches."[2] In the passage quoted above, Arnold describes the method of investigation which the "disinterested" critic should employ in approaching the elusive goal of truth. Essentially, Arnold argues for a recognition of the value of alternative ways of seeking truth. To Arnold, the appreciation of alternatives leads not to a set of inhibiting dogmatic beliefs but a method of investigating them. As John Holloway puts it: "He [Arnold] mediates not a view of the world, but a habit of mind."[3]

Arnold was not the only nineteenth century thinker who valued alternatives, recognized complexity and realized the importance of bringing various perspectives to bear upon a problem. Nor is the relevance of his method of "disinterestedness" confined to nineteenth century investigations and problems. Indeed, what emerges from a study of the dilemma of the talented heroine is not so much a series of answers as a set of alternatives. This study has attempted, in however modest a way, to employ Arnold's method of "disinterestedness"

139

by eschewing an effort at unique and definitive interpretations of the five novels in favor of applying a different perspective--that of "talent"--in the hope of arriving at new insights and alternate ways of viewing the five heroines and their various dilemmas.

We have seen how, like Arnold, Jane Austen, Charlotte Bronte and George Eliot all manifest an appreciation of alternatives. Each author recognizes the conventional, stereotyped expectations which the society of middle-class England held for young women. Such fictional characters as Charlotte Lucas, Lucy Deane and Rosamund Vincy attest to the writers' awareness of social codes for women. But, while these authors are cognizant of the stereotypes, they also present viable alternatives to the conventional female character in the talented heroines: Elizabeth Bennet, Emma Woodhouse, Jane Eyre, Maggie Tulliver and Dorothea Brooke.

While these five heroines share the qualities of intellectual acuity, moral sensitivity and a sense of aspiration, a comparative consideration shows that, among them, they illustrate alternate ways of being talented and alternate facets of the dilemma of talent. Elizabeth Bennet and Emma Woodhouse share the problem of possessing positive but illusory self-images; Maggie Tulliver and Dorothea Brooke suffer from negative self-images; Jane Eyre enjoys the freedom of a positive and healthy self-image. The differing self-images of the five heroines lead them to adopt various kinds of self-definitions with respect to their societies. Some heroines, like Elizabeth and Jane Eyre, assume stances which are openly defiant of social norms. Maggie Tulliver, in her attempted submission to social expectations, illustrates another way of responding to social pressures. Emma and Dorothea react in more complex and less polarized ways: Emma's deceptions and Dorothea's progressing stance illustrate other alternatives to open defiance or complete submission.

Given the great degree of variance in the talented heroines' self-images and self-definitions, it is not surprising that their aspirations vary in quality, intensity and the degree to which they are fulfilled. All of the heroines aspire to the freedom to realize their own self-definitions but, beyond that, their individual particularized aspirations illustrate various aspects of the condition of being a talented woman. Intellectual acuity and moral sensitivity distinguish the talented heroines from the conventional female characters in the novels. But the five talented heroines possess these qualities to different degrees, as the dissimilarity of their personal aspirations illustrates. Dorothea Brooke's aspiration for knowledge, for example, demonstrates how the intellectual acuity of the talented heroine can determine her ambitions while Maggie Tulliver's consuming desire for love and Elizabeth Bennet's yearning for human dignity show how the heroine's moral sensitivity may predispose her to certain kinds of aspirations.

The common dilemma of the talented heroines consists in the fact that they are intelligent, morally sensitive women whose unconventional aspirations place them at odds with the prevailing mores of their respective societies. Each of them is confronted with this basic human dilemma which is exacerbated for them by the condition of being female: How does one reconcile personal aspirations with the demands of a society which is distinctly uncongenial to such aspirations? Not all of the heroines succeed in achieving this reconciliation; some fail and others succeed only partially. But among them they illustrate alternate ways of responding to the perennial human problem of the conflict between the need to be true to oneself and the demands of society.

Elizabeth Bennet and Emma Woodhouse enjoy the enviable situation of simultaneously fulfilling their aspirations and achieving reconciliation with their societies. Elizabeth's aspiration to personal happiness and human freedom is fulfilled through her union with Darcy. When she attains the approval of the important members of her familial society--Jane, Mrs. Bennet and Mr. Bennet-- her happiness is complete and she looks forward to leaving her old society and to entering a new social world with Darcy:

> She looked forward with delight to the time when they
> [Elizabeth and Darcy] should be removed from society so
> little pleasing to either, to all the comfort and elegance of
> their family party at Pemberley. (P & P, 287)

Emma's integration into her society is slightly more complex than Elizabeth's. It begins when Emma attains the self-knowledge which enables her to realize how illusory and yet how harmful has been her image of herself as a benign manipulator. Self-knowledge ultimately leads Emma to knowledge about others: she recognizes the nobility of Mr. Knightley's character and her own unconscious love for him. But before the marriage which symbolizes her reconciliation with her society can take place, Emma must atone for the sorrow which her ambitions to power have caused others. She is punished for her impersonal, insensitive treatment of Harriet Smith by suffering from the mistaken belief that Harriet has won Mr. Knightley's love. Emma's unkindness towards Jane Fairfax must also be expiated through humbling herself to visit Jane and seeking to effect a reconciliation with her. Emma renounces her former aspirations to power but the real state of her aspiration for self-fulfillment is left open. The reader is however, led to assume that Knightley's respect for Emma's intelligence and her basic goodness will enable him to support her in her still unrealized aspiration to fulfill her human potential.

Jane Eyre's situation provides an alternative to the fulfillment of aspiration and the integration into society which Elizabeth Bennet, and to a lesser degree, Emma, enjoy. Like Elizabeth, Jane achieves the sense of personal freedom and dignity to which she had aspired. The reformed Rochester recognizes her integrity and her humanity. He has come to see Jane as "altogether a human being" (*JE*, 385) and Jane's freedom is enriched through a marriage which is based upon love and mutual esteem. Unlike the Austen heroines' however, Jane's marriage is a solitary, not a social, event. No "small band of true friends" (*E*, 335) witnesses this union. Jane tells us: "A quiet wedding we had: he and I, the parson and clerk, were alone present." (*JE*, 395) Jane's solitary wedding and her isolated, a-social life with Rochester are in keeping with Jane's isolated social position throughout most of the novel and with the suspect view of society which informs the novel. There is no Miss Bates in the society of *Jane Eyre* to exclaim, "It is such a happiness when good people get together-- and they always do." (*E*, 117) Rather, social intercourse in *Jane Eyre* is depicted as empty and frivolous in the instance of Rochester's house party; as debasing and amoral in Rochester's sordid tale of his "socially arranged" marriage and subsequent illicit liaisons; or as cruel and indifferent when numerous people spurn the hungry and homeless Jane on her journey away from Thornfield. Because of her orphaned and later, her governess's status, Jane is excluded from society while at the same time she suffers from its repressive codes. Basically, Jane sees herself as a pilgrim journeying through life with providential guidance; her union with Rochester is a-social but completely in harmony with her self-definition.

Elizabeth Bennet, Emma Woodhouse and Jane Eyre illustrate alternate ways in which the talented heroine may fulfill her aspirations. In Maggie Tulliver and Dorothea Brooke George Eliot presents the alternatives of unfulfilled aspiration accompanied by disintegration or by barely adequate integration into society. Maggie Tulliver fails to achieve her personal aspirations for love, learning and beauty. In exercising her freedom to reject Stephen, she fulfills a basic human aspiration to create oneself through free moral choice but she renounces forever her concrete aspirations. Maggie fails also to achieve integration into her larger society. She is reconciled individually with her mother, Philip, Lucy and Tom, but the society of St. Ogg's treats her as a pariah:

> *The ladies of St. Ogg's were not beguiled by any wide speculative conceptions; but they had their favourite abstraction, called Society, which served to make their consciences perfectly easy in doing what satisfied their own egoism--thinking and speaking the worst of Maggie Tulliver, and turning their backs upon her. (MF, 442)*

Eliot can only end Maggie's story with death; and for Eliot exclusion from the living community of humankind is indeed a kind of death. Maggie's end is complete disintegration; she dies with Tom in a literal flood which is also symbolic of her own fatally passionate nature.

The integration of Dorothea Brooke is less obviously tragic than Maggie's but perhaps more poignant. We have seen how Dorothea abandons her heroic aspirations and embraces the "home epic" always feeling "that there was always something better which she might have done, if she had only been better and known better." (M, 610) After her marriage to Will, Dorothea achieves a gradual and incomplete reconciliation with her immediate family. But the larger community of Middlemarch never accepts Dorothea:

> *Sir James never ceased to regard Dorothea's second marriage as a mistake; indeed this remained the tradition concerning it in Middlemarch, where she was spoken of to a younger generation as a fine girl who married a sickly clergyman, old enough to be her father, and in little more than a year after his death gave up her estate to marry his cousin--young enough to have been his son, with no property, and not well-born. Those who had not seen anything of Dorothea usually observed that she could not have been "a nice woman," else she would not have married either the one or the other. (M, 612)*

Indeed, Eliot tells the reader that Dorothea's marital choices were not "ideally beautiful" and this fact has disturbed countless readers and critics who are unsatisfied with the rather weakly delineated character of Will Ladislaw and with Dorothea's marriage to him. It seems likely, however, that Eliot intended the reader to be uncomfortable with Dorothea's fate. Eliot would have us mindful of the essential problem of unfulfillment which constitutes the human condition. While lofty aspirations and heroic goals are admirable, they are not achievable in the unspectacular modern world. One's choice is, ultimately, to attain a workable if uneasy poise, as Dorothea does, or to suffer the disintegration which Maggie experiences.

Considered together, the five heroines illustrate the wide variety of alternative possibilities which are open to the talented woman. Although the five novels under consideration are concerned with women's aspirations, none of them may fairly be called a "feminist" novel. They are not didactic works which attribute the heroines' frustrations solely to society, the opposite sex, conventional religion, or any other external factors. While society may constrain Emma, her faults are her own; while it contributes to Maggie's tragedy, she has the free will to restrain her passions. Ultimately, one turns to Eliot's complex and balanced view: some frustrations are imposed by society, some failures are a result of individual character flaws:

> "1st Gent.   *Our deeds are fetters that we forge ourselves.*
> 2nd Gent.   *Ay, truly: But I think it is the world*
>   *That brings the iron."* (M, 25)

Both talented heroine and hero alike share in the tragedy of incompleteness and imperfection inherent in the human condition because both are located, not in a world of romance or a utopia:

> *But in the very world, which is the world*
> *Of all of us,--the place where, in the end,*
> *We find our happiness, or not at all!*[4]

SUGGESTIONS FOR FURTHER READING

There are a number of recent works which, while not bearing directly upon the subject of this monograph, will be of interest to the student of English literature, women's studies, and nineteenth century social and intellectual history. The reader who desires to expand her/his knowledge of the social and historical realities confronting the Victorian woman would be well advised to consult the following works: Patricia Branca's *Silent Sisterhood: Middle Class Women in the Victorian Home* (Pittsburgh: Carnegie Mellon University Press, 1975); Vineta Colby's *Yesterday's Woman: Domestic Realism in the English Novel* (Princeton: Princeton University Press, 1974); Lenore Davidoff's *The Best Circles: Women and Society in Victorian England* (Totowa, New Jersey: Rowman and Littlefield, 1973); Lee Holcombe's *Victorian Ladies at Work: Middle-Class Working Women in England and Wales, 1850-1914* (Hamden, Conn: Archon Books, 1973); Sheila Rowbotham's *Hidden from History: Rediscovering Women in History from the Seventeenth Century to the Present* (New York: Pantheon Books, 1974); and Katherine Moore's *Victorian Wives* (New York: St. Martin's Press, 1974).

In *Silent Sisterhood*, Patricia Branca ably challenges the familiar stereotypes about the apathy and powerlessness of the nineteenth century woman. Arguing that the Victorian woman was, in a sense, the first "modern" woman, Branca utilizes such primary sources as household manuals, women's periodicals, health care literature and statistical data to demonstrate how the Victorian middle class woman was a crucial agent of modernization. Vineta Colby, in *Yesterday's Woman*, discusses Catherine Gore, Maria Edgeworth, Charlotte Yonge, Harriet Martineau, and other minor women novelists of the nineteenth century. Eschewing a directly feminist perspective, Colby provides a competent analysis of many little known works and contends that these women authors established a mode of domestic realism which was later exploited by the major Victorian novelists. Lenore Davidoff's *The Best Circles* examines Victorian family and social life and new patterns of behavior which began to be codified in the 1820's. Using a historical-sociological approach, Davidoff attempts a new explanation of the stability of Victorian society and shows how elaborate rituals of etiquette were structured both to govern access to nineteenth century society and to ensure the stability of that society. *Victorian Ladies at Work* by Lee Holcombe examines five fields of employment available to the middle class woman--teaching, nursing, shop and office work, and the civil service-- and delineates the barriers faced by the nineteenth century woman in attempting to achieve equality with men in employment opportunities and financial remuneration. A valuable survey of the impact of historical movements on the "hidden" lives of women is provided by Sheila Rowbotham in *Hidden from History*. Employing primary sources, Rowbotham furnishes a lively account of the reality of women's lives in Victorian England. Katherine Moore's *Victorian Wives* is an interesting study of English and American Victorian wives in fact and fiction. Less scholarly and more general in approach than the works cited above, Moore's work is a series of informal, genial essays which comment upon how specific Victorian wives either fulfilled or reacted against the stereotyped expectations of their respective societies.

The Women's Liberation Movement has sparked a new and scholarly interest in the long overlooked area of female sexuality. Rosalind Miles, in *The Fiction of Sex: Themes and Functions of Sex Difference in the Modern Novel* (New York: Barnes and Noble, 1975) discusses the concept of sexuality in the nineteenth and twentieth century English and American novel. *Sex and Marriage in Victorian Poetry*, by Wendell Stacy Johnson (Ithaca and London: Cornell University Press, 1975) undercuts the conventional stereotype of the prudish, repressed, conventional Victorian and examines the sexual, social, and aesthetic meanings which the major Victorian poets found in marriage and expressed in their writings. Like Johnson, Eric Trudgill, in *Madonnas and Magdalens: The Origins and Development of Victorian Sexual Attitudes* (New York: Holmes and Meier, 1976), argues that the Victorians have been unfairly condemned as narrow-minded and hypocritical. Demonstrating how nineteenth century English sexual attitudes were neither hypocritical nor static, Trudgill explores the historical, social, and theological sources of Victorian sexual attitudes and traces their evolution from the mid-eighteenth to the early twentieth century. In *The Physician and Sexuality in Victorian America* (Urbana: University of Illinois Press, 1974) John S. Haller, Jr. and Robin M. Haller show how stereotypes of women which prevailed in England were also operative in America. Utilizing primary sources from the medical field, this enlightening and well documented study examines physicians' beliefs in the inferiority of women and the effects of these attitudes upon their treatment of women and upon their patients' self-images.

A number of worthwhile studies concern themselves with women writers and with images of women in fiction. Elaine Showalter's *A Literature of Their Own: British Women Novelists from Bronte to Lessing* (Princeton: Princeton University Press, 1977) and Ellen Moers' *Literary Women* (New York: Doubleday, 1976) are especially remarkable for their comprehensive range, scholarly approach, and stimulating literary style. Showalter brilliantly demonstrates how the female tradition in English literature has gone through three distinct phases: the Feminine (marked by imitation of modes of the dominant literary tradition); the Feminist (notable for protest against traditional standards and values); and the Female (marked by a sense of self-discovery and a search for identity). Tracing the evolution of the female tradition through these phases from 1800 to the present, Showalter considers such figures as Charlotte Bronte, George Eliot, Mary Braddon, Olive Schreiner, Virginia Woolf, Margaret Drabble, Doris Lessing and many minor female writers. *A Literature of Their Own* is carefully researched and painstakingly documented; it includes a useful biographical appendix and a full bibliography.

Ellen Moers' *Literary Women* discusses nineteenth and twentieth century English, American, and French female writers. Moers provides a stimulating account of the literary climate which surrounded the nineteenth century woman writer, and her work includes a provocative discussion of Freudian symbolism in the novels of such female writers as George Sand, George Eliot, and Willa Cather. Illuminating the significance of women's literary relations with one another, Moers argues competently and incisively that a major part of the female literary heritage is the tradition of women writers looking to the writings of other women for nourishment and support.

Three recent works by Francoise Basch, Patricia Beer and Jenni Calder, respectively, deal with images of women in Victorian fiction. In *Relative Creatures: Victorian Women in Society and the Novel*, translated by Anthony Rudolf (New York: Schocken Books, 1974), Basch uses the data of novelists and social historians to study the restrictive and oppressive conditions which shaped Victorian women and their fictional counterparts from 1837 to 1867. Beer's *Reader, I Married Him* (London: Macmillan, 1975; New York: Barnes and Noble, 1974) examines female characters in the fiction of Jane Austen, Charlotte Bronte, Elizabeth Gaskell and George Eliot. Viewing the women novelists' portrayals of female characters as specifically dominated by the search for a mate, Beer discusses the attitudes towards the female condition which each author expresses through her characters. In *Women and Marriage in Victorian Fiction* (New York: Oxford University Press, 1976), Jenni Calder surveys the treatment of marriage and the family in the works of major Victorian novelists from Thackeray to Hardy. Using biographical data and sociological studies to investigate novels and ideologies of the Victorian period, Calder shows how stereotyped attitudes towards women affected the moral and artistic development of contemporary writers.

Two insightful collections of feminist critical essays are Elizabeth Hardwick's *Seduction and Betrayal: Women and Literature* (New York: Random House, 1974) and *Images of Women in Fiction: Feminist Perspectives* (Bowling Green, Ohio: Bowling Green University Popular Press, 1972) edited by Susan Koppelman Cornillon. The first work discusses the lives and situations of women authors, women relatives of authors, and women characters in fiction. The social factors which inhibited such women as Charlotte Bronte, Ibsen's Nora, Hedda, and Rebecca West, Zelda Fitzgerald, Sylvia Plath, Virginia Woolf, Dorothy Wordsworth and Jane Carlyle are thoughtfully analyzed while the title essay explores the literary theme of the heroine who is seduced, betrayed, and ennobled by subsequent sufferings. Cornillon's collection utilizes such useful categories as "The Woman as Heroine," "The Invisible Woman," and "The Woman as Hero" to investigate the traditional views of women in nineteenth and twentieth century American and English novels, the stereotyped woman in fiction and fiction in which women writers discover themselves, their independence, and their creativity.

The concepts of literary femininity and creativity are explored by Patricia Meyer Spacks and Lisa Appignanesi in their respective works. Spacks' *The Female Imagination* (New York: Knopf Press, 1975) is a useful survey which investigates female self-awareness in such writers as Alcott, de Beauvoir, the Brontes, Lessing, Nin, Wharton, and Woolf. *Femininity and the Creative Imagination* by Lisa Appignanesi (New York: Barnes and Noble, 1973) is a comparative study of Henry James, Robert Musil and Marcel Proust which analyzes the "myth of femininity" and the link between femininity and creativity.

Images of women in American and British literature are treated in three valuable studies. Judith Fryer, in *The Faces of Eve: Women in the Nineteenth Century American Novel* (New York: Oxford University Press, 1977), studies the facets of the Eve figure in nineteenth century American literature: woman as "Temptress, American Princess, Great Mother and New Woman." This able analysis of women in the works of Hawthorne, Melville, Oliver Wendell Holmes, James, and Howells is supplemented by extensive footnotes and a comprehensive bibliography. *Feminine Consciousness in the Modern British Novel* by Sydney Janet Kaplan (Urbana, Chicago, London: University of Illinois Press, 1975) examines twenty-five British women writers and explores the feminine consciousness in the women characters of female writers. Mary Allen's *The Necessary Blankness: Women in Major American Fiction of the Sixties* (Urbana, Chicago, London: University of Illinois Press, 1976) investigates visions of women in the works of such novelists as Philip Roth, John Updike, John Barth, Thomas Pynchon, Joyce Carol Oates and Sylvia Plath. Reminding us, perhaps, that the stereotyping of women in fiction is not unique to the Victorians, Allen concludes from her study of American literature in the sixties that fictional women of that period are almost uniformly "blank" creatures--passive, dependent and vulnerable.

These suggestions for further reading are meant to serve the interested reader and possibly to function as a point of departure for the beginning researcher of nineteenth century women, women in literature, and women's studies generally. No claim to comprehensiveness or exhaustiveness is implied by this essay. For example, a number of recent and excellent biographies of significant women writers do not fall within the purview of this bibliographical treatment. Indeed, there is such a wealth of valuable studies on women, women novelists and women in fiction, both currently available and constantly forthcoming, that initiates to this field of research are likely to feel somewhat overwhelmed by the rich store of scholarly materials that are now obtainable. The reader would be well advised to consult the new *International Journal of Women's Studies* which is doubtlessly destined to provide yet another important outlet for articles, reviews and notices on women's studies from a broad international community of readers and contributors. Lastly, the annual bibliographies published by the Modern Language Association, *Victorian Studies*, and reviews in *PMLA*, *Victorian Studies, Victorian Poetry* and *Women's Studies* are highly recommended to the reader who wishes to pursue the complex and multi-faceted topic of women in literature.

Susan E. Siefert
Alverno College
1977

149

NOTES

Chapter 1

[1] George Eliot, *Middlemarch*, ed. Gordon S. Haight (Boston: Houghton Mifflin Co., Riverside Press, 1956), p. 4. All subsequent references to this edition will be cited within the body of the text.

[2] See W. Lyon Blease, *The Emancipation of English Women* (London: Constable & Co., 1910); C. Willett Cunnington, *Feminine Attitudes in the Nineteenth Century* (New York: Macmillan Co., 1936); Janet Dunbar, *The Early Victorian Woman: Some Aspects of Her Life 1837-1857* (London: Theodore Bruin, 1953); John Langdon-Davies, *A Short History of Women* (New York: Viking Press, 1927); Hazel Mews, *Frail Vessels: Women's Role in Women's Novels from Fanny Burney to George Eliot* (London: Athlone Press, 1969); Wanda Fraiken Neff, *Victorian Working Women* (New York: Columbia University Press, 1929); Ruth M. Adams, "The Victorian Woman in Fact and Fiction 1871-1901" (Ph.D. dissertation, Radcliffe College, 1951); Bernice Davies, "The Social Status of the Middle Class Victorian Woman as it is Interpreted in Representative Mid-Nineteenth Century Novels and Periodicals" (Ph.D. dissertation, Stanford University, 1943); Louise Rorabacher, "Victorian Women in Life and in Fiction" (Ph.D. dissertation, University of Illinois, 1942); Zea Zinn, "Love and Marriage in the Novels of English Women: 1740-1840" (Ph.D. dissertation, University of Wisconsin, 1935).

[3] Louise E. Rorabacher, "Victorian Women in Life and in Fiction" (Ph.D. dissertation, University of Illinois, 1942), pp. 11-31.

[4] "In Great Britain in 1851 there were 2,765,000 single women aged 15 and over. By 1861 this figure had risen to 2,956,000 and by 1871 to 3,228,700 --an increase of 16.8 per cent over the twenty years. . . . these figures contained an increase of from 72,500 to 125,200 *surplus* single women, or 72.7 per cent over the twenty years." J.A. and Olive Banks, *Feminism and Family Planning*

in Victorian England (New York: Schocken Books, 1964), p. 27.

[5] Wanda Fraiken Neff, *Victorian Working Women* (New York: Columbia University Press, 1929), p. 190.

[6] William M. Thackeray, *Vanity Fair*, ed. Geoffrey and Kathleen Tillotson (Boston: Houghton Mifflin Co., Riverside Press, 1963), p. 12. Thackeray's heroine, Amelia, received this accomplished "education" when "the present century was in its teens," but finishing schools changed little throughout the century. In 1872 a magazine writer lamented "the hopeless inadequacy of most of the ladies' schools where only accomplishments to increase a girl's attractions before marriage are taught; at present it is almost a misfortune for women to have aspirations and culture higher than the ordinary level; most women have not yet arrived at the point of realising their ignorance and subserviency, and many are merely gilt drawing-room ornaments." C. Willett Cunnington, *Feminine Attitudes in the Nineteenth Century* (New York: Macmillan Co., 1936), pp. 227-228.

[7] Patricia Thomson, *The Victorian Heroine: A Changing Ideal 1837-1873* (London: Oxford University Press, 1956), p. 10.

[8] *Ibid.*, p. 10.

[9] *A Father's Legacy to His Daughters*, quoted in John Langdon-Davies, *A Short History of Women* (New York: Viking Press, 1927), p. 331.

[10] *Ibid.*, pp. 332-333.

[11] *Ibid.*, p. 332.

[12] Walter Houghton, *The Victorian Frame of Mind 1830-1870*(New Haven: Yale University Press, 1957), p. 341.

[13] Coventry Patmore, "The Married Lover," in *Poems By Coventry Patmore* (London: George Bell & Son, 1897), lines 1-8.

[14] *The Princess*, pt. 7, lines 301-302.

[15] Mary Wollstonecraft, *A Vindication of the Rights of Woman*, ed. Charles W. Hagelman, Jr. (New York: W.W. Norton & Co., 1967), pp. 93-94.

[16] Matthew Arnold, *Essays in Criticism*, with an Introduction by G.K. Chesterton (London: J.M. Dent & Sons, 1964), p. 93.

[17] *Ibid.*, p. 91.

[18] *Ibid.*, p. 92.

[19] Jane Austen, *Pride and Prejudice*, ed. Mark Schorer. (Boston: Houghton Mifflin Co., Riverside Press, 1956), p. 24. All subsequent references to this edition will be cited within the body of the text.

[20] George Eliot, *The Mill on the Floss*, ed. Gordon S. Haight (Boston: Houghton Mifflin Co., Riverside Press, 1956), p. 12. All subsequent references to this edition will be cited within the body of the text.

[21] Jane Austen, *Emma*, ed. Stephen M. Parrish (New York: W.W. Norton

& Co., 1972), p. 28. All subsequent references to this edition will be cited within the body of the text.

[22] Charlotte Bronte, *Jane Eyre*, ed. Richard J. Dunn (New York: W.W. Norton & Co., 1971), p. 109. All subsequent references to this edition will be cited within the body of the text.

[23] Perhaps surprisingly, horseback riding was considered to be a desirable accomplishment for ladies. Zea Zinn notes: "Outdoor sports were unheard of for girls, walking and riding being the only possible forms of exercise." "Love and Marriage in the Novels of English Women: 1740-1840" (Ph.D. dissertation, University of Wisconsin, 1935), p. 18. George Eliot shows Rosamund displaying her figure in her riding habit (*M*, 87) while the ascetic Dorothea rejects Sir James Chettam's notion that "Every lady ought to be a perfect horsewoman, that she may accompany her husband." (*M*, 16)

[24] Marvin Mudrick, *Jane Austen: Irony as Defense and Discovery* (Berkeley, University of California Press, 1968), p. 109.

[25] Janet Dunbar, *The Early Victorian Woman: Some Aspects of Her Life 1837-1857* (London: Theodore Bruin, 1953), p. 22.

[26] Mark Schorer, "The Humiliation of Emma Woodhouse," *The Literary Review* 2 (Summer 1959): 547-563, rpt. in *Jane Austen: A Collection of Critical Essays*, ed. Ian Watt (Englewood Cliffs, New Jersey: Prentice-Hall, 1963), p. 107.

Chapter 2

[1] William Cowper, *The Task*, Book IV, "The Winter Evening," quoted in Jane Austen, *Emma*, ed. Stephen M. Parrish (New York: W.W. Norton & Co., 1972), p. 234. Emphasis added.

[2] D.W. Harding, "Regulated Hatred: An Aspect of the Work of Jane Austen," *Scrutiny* 8 (1940): 346-362, rpt. in *Jane Austen: A Collection of Critical Essays*, ed. Ian Watt (Englewood Cliffs, New Jersey: Prentice-Hall, 1963), p. 172.

[3] Howard Babb, *Jane Austen's Novels: The Fabric of Dialogue* (Columbus, Ohio: Ohio State University Press, 1962), p. 115.

[4] R.W. Chapman, ed. *Jane Austen's Letters to Her Sister Cassandra*, 2nd edition (London, 1952), quoted in Jane Austen, *Pride and Prejudice*, ed. Donald J. Gray (New York: W.W. Norton & Co., 1966), p. 280.

[5] Jane Austen, *Emma*, ed. Stephen M. Parrish (New York: W.W. Norton & Co., 1972), p. viii.

[6] A. Walton Litz, *Jane Austen: A Study of Her Artistic Development*

152

(New York: Oxford University Press, 1965), p. 142.

[7] G. Armour Craig, "The Unpoetic Compromise: On the Relation Between Private Vision and the Social Order in Nineteenth-Century English Fiction," in *Self and Society in the Novel*, ed. Mark Schorer (New York: Columbia University Press, 1956), pp. 30-41, rpt. in Charlotte Bronte, *Jane Eyre*, ed. Richard J. Dunn (New York: W.W. Norton & Co., 1971), p. 447.

Chapter 3

[1] Some critics have seen Maggie's choice to renounce Stephen and return to Tom and his values as a sign of maturity and development. William H. Marshall, for example, notes that by Maggie's "total commitment to Tom in moments before their death, to which she has brought the force of all her experiences since childhood, she achieves an instant of realization of 'that mysterious wondrous happiness that is one with pain.' (Bk. VII, Ch. V.) Quite clearly, Maggie has attained the realization of the self that she has sought, and for one moment she has assimilated the past into the present." *The World of the Victorian Novel* (Cranbury, New Jersey: A.S. Barnes & Co., 1967), p. 89.

Chapter 4

[1] Gabriel Marcel, *The Philosophy of Existentialism*, trans. Manya Harari (New York: The Citadel Press, 1966), pp. 9-12.

[2] The term functionalism is employed by the social sciences to describe any doctrine that emphasizes purpose, practical utility, or adaptiveness. I am not here using the term in this established sense. Rather, for the purposes of this discussion, "functionalism" is employed as a convenient term which summarizes the effects of the "functionalised" world of which Gabriel Marcel speaks. Hence, the word "functionalism" shall appear in quotation marks in order to distinguish my usage from the more precise way in which the social scientist would use this term.

[3] The increased prosperity of the middle class which resulted from the industrial revolution contributed indirectly to the loss of the middle-class woman's identity. Prior to 1837, a young lady gave up her life of "visiting, novel-reading, gossiping and embroidering" for the married woman's duties of household management. But with the easy accessibility of servants, and the material prosperity which enabled the middle class to employ large numbers of

them, housewifery had fallen into disrepute. By 1837, "not only the marriage-able girls in a house but also its mistress were casting helplessly around for something to do, something to occupy their vacant hours–something, however, that would not distract from their new standing as Middle-Class Ladies." Essentially, the extent of his wife and daughters' idleness provided an index of the business success of the husband and father of the family. The middle-class woman was hence deprived of any socially useful role; her function was, through her languor and idleness, to provide an outward symbol of her men-folk's material success. Patricia Thomson, *The Victorian Heroine: A Changing Ideal 1837-1873* (London: Oxford University Press, 1956), p. 14.

[4] M. Jeanne Peterson, "The Victorian Governess: Status Incongruence in Family and Society," in *Suffer and Be Still: Women in the Victorian Age*, ed. Martha Vicinus (Bloomington: Indiana University Press, 1972), p. 11.

[5] Duncan Crow, *The Victorian Woman* (New York: Stein and Day, 1972), p. 204.

[6] Zea Zinn, "Love and Marriage in the Novels of English Women: 1740-1840" (Ph.D. dissertation, University of Wisconsin, 1935), p. 15. The extent to which a married woman's identity was submerged in her husband's is indi-cated by her legal status: "She could neither own property nor make a will, keep her own savings nor claim any of her husband's. By marriage she lost her identity in his and consequently had no power over her children and no grounds for divorce . . ." Patricia Thomson, *The Victorian Heroine*, p. 13.

[7] Mrs. Sarah Stickney Ellis, *The Women of England* (London: Fisher, Son, & Co., 1839), pp. 241-242.

[8] *Ibid.*, p. 249.

[9] *Ibid.*, p. 221.

[10] *Ibid.*, p. 215.

[11] "From November to March, fine ladies were laid up, so to speak, for the winter, almost as thoroughly as bicycles used to be laid up. It will perhaps be remembered how Jane Austen's charming heroine Elizabeth Bennet, aston-ished and indeed scandalized her friends by her spirited walking in the mud." M. Phillips and W.S. Tomkinson, *English Women in Life and Letters* (Oxford: Oxford University Press, 1927), pp. 129-130.

[12] *A Father's Legacy to His Daughters*, quoted in John Langdon-Davies, *A Short History of Women* (New York: Viking Press, 1927), p. 331.

[13] John Langdon-Davies, *A Short History of Women*, p. 374.

[14] Mrs. Sarah Stickney Ellis, *The Women of England*, p. 221.

[15] W. Lyon Blease, *The Emancipation of English Women* (London: Constable & Co., 1910), p. 69.

[16] Derek Oldfield, "The Character of Dorothea," in *Middlemarch: Critical Approaches to the Novel*, ed. Barbara Hardy (London: Athlone Press, 1967), pp. 78-79.

[17] C. Willett Cunnington, *Feminine Attitudes in the Nineteenth Century* (New York: Macmillan Co., 1936), p. 110.

[18] Patricia Thomson, *The Victorian Heroine*, p. 37.

[19] *Quarterly Review* 84 (December 1848): 180, quoted in Wanda Fraiken Neff, *Victorian Working Women* (New York: Columbia University Press, 1929), pp. 154-155.

[20] *Quarterly Review* 84 (December 1848): 177, quoted in Wanda Fraiken Neff, *Victorian Working Women*, p. 167.

[21] M. Jeanne Peterson, "The Victorian Governess," in *Suffer and Be Still*, ed. Martha Vicinus, p. 13.

[22] *Ibid.*, p. 210.

[23] *Governess Life: Its Trials, Duties, and Encouragements* (London, 1849), p. 127, quoted in M. Jeanne Peterson, "The Victorian Governess," in *Suffer and Be Still*, ed. Martha Vicinus, p. 15.

[24] M. Jeanne Peterson, "The Victorian Governess," in *Suffer and Be Still*, ed. Martha Vicinus, p. 15.

[25] *Ibid.*, p. 4.

[26] Patricia Thomson, *The Victorian Heroine*, p. 37.

[27] Bernice F. Davies, "The Social Status of the Middle Class Victorian Woman as it is Interpreted in Representative Mid-Nineteenth Century Novels and Periodicals" (Ph.D. dissertation, Stanford University, 1943), p. 21.

[28] *A Father's Legacy*, quoted in John Langdon-Davies, *A Short History of Women*, pp. 333-334.

[29] Gabriel Marcel, *The Philosophy of Existentialism*, p. 10.

Chapter 5

[1] Gabriel Marcel, *The Philosophy of Existentialism*, trans. Manya Harari (New York: The Citadel Press, 1966), p. 26.

[2] *Ibid.*, p. 14.

[3] Zea Zinn, "Love and Marriage in the Novels of English Women: 1740-1840" (Ph.D. dissertation, University of Wisconsin, 1935), p. 113.

[4] Stuart M. Tave, *Some Words of Jane Austen* (Chicago: University of Chicago Press, 1973), p. 33.

[5] *Quarterly Review* 84 (December 1848): 173-174, in Judith O'Neill, ed., *Critics on Charlotte and Emily Bronte* (Coral Gables, Florida: University

of Miami Press, 1968), p. 15.

[6] Richard Chase, "The Brontes, or Myth Domesticated," in *Forms of Modern Fiction*, ed. William V. O'Connor (Minneapolis: University of Minnesota Press, 1948), pp. 102-113, rpt. in Charlotte Bronte, *Jane Eyre*, ed. Richard J. Dunn (New York: W.W. Norton & Co., 1971), p. 468.

[7] Robert Bernard Martin, *Charlotte Bronte's Novels: The Accents of Persuasion* (New York: W.W. Norton & Co., 1968), p. 93.

Chapter 6

[1] Matthew Arnold, *Essays in Criticism*, with an Introduction by G.K. Chesterton (London: J.M. Dent & Sons, 1964), p. 3.

[2] *Ibid.*, p. 20.

[3] John Holloway, *The Victorian Sage* (New York: W.W. Norton & Co., 1965), p. 207.

[4] *The Prelude*, bk. 11, lines 142-144.

SELECTED BIBLIOGRAPHY

Primary Sources

Austen, Jane. *Emma*. Edited by Stephen M. Parrish. New York: W.W. Norton & Co., 1972.

——. *Pride and Prejudice*. Edited with an Introduction by Mark Schorer. Boston: Houghton Mifflin Co., Riverside Press, 1956.

Bronte, Charlotte. *Jane Eyre*. Edited by Richard J. Dunn. New York: W.W. Norton & Co., 1971.

Eliot, George. *Middlemarch*. Edited with an Introduction by Gordon S. Haight. Boston: Houghton Mifflin Co., Riverside Press, 1956.

——. *The Mill on the Floss*. Edited with an Introduction by Gordon S. Haight. Boston: Houghton Mifflin Co., Riverside Press, 1956.

Secondary Sources

Adams, Ruth M. "The Victorian Woman in Fact and Fiction 1871-1901." Ph. D. dissertation. Radcliffe College, 1951.

Arnold, Matthew. *Essays in Criticism*. Introduction by G.K Chesterton. London: J.M. Dent & Sons, 1964.

Babb, Howard. *Jane Austen's Novels: The Fabric of Dialogue*. Columbus, Ohio: Ohio State University Press, 1962.

Banks, J.A. and Olive. *Feminism and Family Planning in Victorian England*. New York: Schocken Books, 1964.

Bennett, Joan. *George Eliot: Her Mind and Her Art*. Cambridge: Cambridge University Press, l966.

Blease, W. Lyon. *The Emancipation of English Women*. London: Constable & Co., 1910.

Booth, Wayne. *The Rhetoric of Fiction*. Chicago: University of Chicago Press, 1961.

Burn, W.L. *The Age of Equipoise: A Study of the Mid-Victorian Generation*. New York: W.W. Norton & Co., 1965.

Chase, Richard. "The Brontes, or Myth Domesticated." In Charlotte Bronte, *Jane Eyre*, pp. 462-471. Edited by Richard J. Dunn. New York: W.W. Norton & Co., 1971.

Craig, G. Armour. "Private Vision and Social Order in *Jane Eyre*." In Charlotte Bronte, *Jane Eyre*, pp. 471-478. Edited by Richard J. Dunn. New York: W.W. Norton & Co., 1971.

Crow, Duncan. *The Victorian Woman*. New York: Stein & Day, 1972.

Cunnington, C. Willett. *Feminine Attitudes in the Nineteenth Century*. New York: Macmillan Co., 1936.

Davies, Bernice F. "The Social Status of the Middle Class Victorian Woman as it is Interpreted in Representative Mid-Nineteenth Century Novels and Periodicals." Ph.D. dissertation. Stanford University, 1943.

Dunbar, Janet. *The Early Victorian Woman: Some Aspects of Her Life 1837-1857*. London: Theodore Bruin, 1953.

Ellis, Mrs. Sarah Stickney. *The Women of England, Their Social Duties, and Domestic Habits*. London: Fisher, Son, & Co., 1839.

Friedan, Betty. *The Feminine Mystique*. New York: W.W. Norton & Co., 1963.

Gerin, Winifred. *Charlotte Bronte: The Evolution of Genius*. London: Oxford University Press, 1969.

Haight, Gordon S. *George Eliot: A Biography*. New York: Oxford University Press, 1968.

Harding, D.W. "Regulated Hatred: An Aspect of the Work of Jane Austen." In *Jane Austen: A Collection of Critical Essays*, pp. 166-179. Edited by Ian Watt. Englewood Cliffs, New Jersey: Prentice-Hall, 1963.

Hardy, Barbara. *The Appropriate Form: An Essay on the Novel*. London: Athlone Press, 1964.

———. *The Novels of George Eliot: A Study in Form*. New York: Oxford University Press, 1967.

———. ed. *Middlemarch: Critical Approaches to the Novel*. London: Athlone Press, 1967.

Harvey, W.J. *The Art of George Eliot*. London: Chatto & Windus, 1961.

Holloway, John. *The Victorian Sage: Studies in Argument*. New York: W.W. Norton & Co., 1965.

Houghton, Walter. *The Victorian Frame of Mind 1830-1870*. New Haven: Yale University Press, 1957.

Kroeber, Karl. *Styles in Fictional Structure*. Princeton, New Jersey: Princeton University Press, 1971.

Langdon-Davies, John. *A Short History of Women*. New York: Viking Press, 1927.

Lascelles, Mary. *Jane Austen and Her Art*. London: Oxford University Press, 1963.

Litz, A. Walton. *Jane Austen: A Study of Her Artistic Development*. New York: Oxford University Press, 1965.

Marcel, Gabriel. *The Philosophy of Existentialism*. Translated by Manya Harari. New York: Citadel Press, 1966.

Marshall, William H. *The World of the Victorian Novel*. Cranbury, New Jersey: A.S. Barnes & Co., 1967.

Martin, Robert. *Charlotte Bronte's Novels: The Accents of Persuasion*. New York: W.W. Norton & Co., 1968.

Mews, Hazel. *Frail Vessels: Women's Role in Women's Novels from Fanny Burney to George Eliot*. London: Athlone Press, 1969.

Mudrick, Marvin. *Jane Austen: Irony as Defense and Discovery*. Berkeley: University of California Press, 1968.

Neff, Wanda Fraiken. *Victorian Working Women*. New York: Columbia University Press, 1929.

O'Neill, Judith, ed. *Critics on Charlotte and Emily Bronte*. Coral Gables, Florida: University of Miami Press, 1968.

Peterson, M. Jeanne. "The Victorian Governess: Status Incongruence in Family and Society." In *Suffer and Be Still: Women in the Victorian Age*, pp. 3-19. Edited by Martha Vicinus. Bloomington: Indiana University Press, 1972.

Phillips, M., and Tomkinson, W.S. *English Women in Life and Letters*. Oxford: Oxford University Press, 1927.

Rorabacher, Louise. "Victorian Women in Life and in Fiction." Ph.D. dissertation. University of Illinois, 1942.

Schorer, Mark. "The Humiliation of Emma Woodhouse." In *Jane Austen: A Collection of Critical Essays*, pp. 98-111. Edited by Ian Watt. Englewood Cliffs, New Jersey: Prentice-Hall, 1963.

Stump, Reva. *Movement and Vision in George Eliot's Novels*. Seattle: University of Washington Press, 1959.

Tave, Stuart. *Some Words of Jane Austen*. Chicago: University of Chicago Press, 1973.

Thale, Jerome. *The Novels of George Eliot*. New York: Columbia University Press, 1959.

159

Thomson, Patricia. *The Victorian Heroine: A Changing Ideal 1837-1873*. London: Oxford University Press, 1956.

Tillotson, Kathleen. *Novels of the Eighteen-Forties*. London: Oxford University Press, 1961.

Van Ghent, Dorothy. *The English Novel: Form and Function*. New York: Harper & Row, 1953; Perennial Library, 1967.

Vicinus, Martha, ed. *Suffer and Be Still: Women in the Victorian Age*. Bloomington: Indiana University Press, 1972.

Watt, Ian, ed. *Jane Austen: A Collection of Critical Essays*. Englewood Cliffs, New Jersey: Prentice-Hall, 1963.

Wollstonecraft, Mary. *A Vindication of the Rights of Woman*. Edited with an Introduction by Charles W. Hagelman, Jr. New York: W.W. Norton & Co., 1967.

Zinn, Zea. "Love and Marriage in the Novels of English Women: 1740-1840." Ph.D. dissertation, University of Wisconsin, 1935.

INDEX

Allen, Mary, 149

"Angel in the House, The," 4-5

Appignanesi, Lisa, 148

Arnold, Matthew, 6, 139

Austen, Jane, 6, 31-32; sense of alternatives of, 140; and society in *Emma*, 127; view of happiness of, 115; view of love of, 121; view of marriage of, 77. *See·also* Bennet, Elizabeth (heroine), *Emma, Pride and Prejudice,* Woodhouse, Emma (heroine)

Babb, Howard, 29

Basch, Francoise, 147

Beer, Patricia, 147-148

Bennet, Elizabeth (heroine): 7, 8; aspirations of, 113, 114, 115-122, 141; compared to Charlotte Lucas, 11-12, 114-116; compared to Emma Woodhouse, 31, 37, 114; compared to Jane Bennet, 10; compared to Jane Eyre, 38-39, 44, 114-115, 121; as lacking accomplishment, 9, 70-71; marriage and, 12-13, 76; self-definition of, 66, 69-73, 114, 118; self-image of, 21, 22, 24-30, 46-47, 140; society and, 68-69, 101. *See also Pride and Prejudice*

Best Circles, The, 145-146

Branca, Patricia, 145

Bronte, Charlotte, 6, 39, 140. *See also* Eyre, Jane (heroine) and *Jane Eyre* (novel)

Brooke, Dorothea (heroine): aspirations of, 113, 114, 132-136, 140-141; compared to Celia Brooke, 16-17; compared to Elizabeth Bennet, 90, 91; compared to Emma Woodhouse, 90, 91; compared to Maggie Tulliver, 56, 57, 59, 90; compared to Rosamund Vincy, 15-16; compared to Saint Theresa, 6; as lacking accomplishments, 9; self-definition of, 66, 68, 69,

89-99; self-image of, 21, 24, 46-53; society and, 21-22, 101, 143-144. *See also Middlemarch*

Calder, Jenni, 147, 148
Colby, Vineta, 145
Cornillon, Susan Koppelman, 148

Daughters of England, The, 64
Davidoff, Lenore, 154-146

Eastlake, Lady, 122
Eliot, George. *See* Evans, Marian
Ellis, Sarah Stickney, 64, 66-68, 69, 92, 94
Emma (novel), 42; art in, 42; dilemma of talent in, 21; the governess in, 102-103; marriage in, 75-78; society in, 78-80, 91, 127-130, 131-132 passim. *See also* Woodhouse, Emma (heroine)
Evans, Marian [psued. George Eliot] : awareness of complexity of, 22; and character of Dorothea Brooke, 89; concern with "indefiniteness" of, 7; description of egoism of, 32; feminine stereotypes and, 1-2; personal freedom in heroines of, 132; sense of alternatives of, 140; treatment of Rosamund Vincy in, 15; treatment of self-image in, 45-46; use of saint motif in, 6; view of society of, 144. *See also* Brooke, Dorothea (heroine), *Middlemarch, Mill on the Floss, The*, Tulliver, Maggie (heroine)
Eyre, Jane (heroine), 7; aspirations of, 113, 114, 122-127; compared to Austen's heroines, 39, 44; compared to Dorothea Brooke, 99, 106, 107, 108, 110; compared to Elizabeth Bennet, 99, 106, 108, 110, 114-115, 121; compared to Emma Woodhouse, 99, 106, 108, 110; compared to Maggie Tulliver, 109-110, 114; compared to Reed sisters, 17-20 passim; as lacking accomplishments, 9; marriage and, 76; self-definition of, 66-68, 69, 99-111, 114, 126; self-image of, 21, 22-23, 38-44, 61, 140; society and, 142. *See also Jane Eyre* (novel)

Faces of Eve, The 148-149
Female Imagination, The, 148
Feminine Consciousness in the Modern British Novel, 149
Feminine Mystique, The, 63
Femininity and the Creative Imagination, 148
Fiction of Sex, The, 146
Friedan, Betty, 63
Fryer, Judith, 148-149

Governess: in *Emma*, 102-103; in *Jane Eyre*, 103-107, 111; in *Middlemarch*, 103; in *Pride and Prejudice*, 102; in Victorian society, 100-102, 104
Great Expectations, 63
Gregory, Dr., 3-4, 64, 76, 106

Haller, John S., Jr., 146
Haller, Robin, 146
Hardwick, Elizabeth, 148
Hidden from History, 145, 146
Holcombe, Lee, 145, 146
Holloway, John, 139

Images of Women in Fiction, 148
International Journal of Women's Studies, 149

Jane Eyre, (novel), 20; aspiration in, 124-125; as autobiography, 39; freedom in, 122-124; governess in, 104; marriage in, 43-44, 106-109; religious imagery in, 125-126; society in, 100. *See also* Eyre, Jane (heroine)
Johnson, Wendell Stacy, 146

Kaplan, Sydney Janet, 149

Langdon-Davies, John, 85
Legacy to My Daughters, 3-4
Literary Women, 147
Literature of Their Own, A, 147

Madonnas and Magdalens, 146
Marcel, Gabriel, 62, 98, 112-113
Marriage: as competition, 2, 8; in *Emma*, 33, 35, 75-78; in *Jane Eyre*, 43-44, 106-109; in *Middlemarch*, 15, 49-53, 134, 143; in *Mill on the Floss, The*, 86, 88-89, 137; in nineteenth century society, 13, 64-65, 119; in *Pride and Prejudice*, 11-13, 26-28, 115-121
"Married Lover, The," 4-5
Middlemarch: Dorothea Brooke in, 16, 53; feminine stereotypes in, 1-2, 8; the governess in, 103; marriage in, 65, 92, 94-98, 134, 143; Rosamund Vincy in, 9, 15-16; saint motif in, 6; self-image in, 45-46; society in, 94, 96, 99, 144. *See also* Brooke, Dorothea (heroine)
Miles, Rosalind, 146

163

Mill on the Floss, The, 17, 53; ending of, 56-57, 153 n.l.; free choice in, 138; marriage in, 65; society in, 66, 86-89. *See also* Tulliver, Maggie (heroine)
Moers, Ellen, 147
Moore, Katherine, 145, 146
Mothers of England, 64

Necessary Blankness, The, 149

Oldfield, Derek, 97

Patmore, Coventry, 4-5
Philosophy of Existentialism, The, 62
Physician and Sexuality in Victorian America, The, 146-147
Pride and Prejudice: ending of, 68-69, 73; the governess in, 102; happiness in, 115, 120; marriage in, 11-13, 65, 68, 69, 71-72, 115-121; society in, 115-119 passim. *See also* Bennet, Elizabeth (heroine)
Princess, The, 5

Quarterly Review, The, 100, 106

Reader, I Married Him, 147-148
Relative Creatures, 147
Rowbotham, Sheila, 145, 146

St. Theresa of Avila, 6, 135, 136
Seduction and Betrayal, 148
Sex and Marriage in Victorian Poetry, 146
Showalter, Elaine, 147
Silent Sisterhood, 145
Spacks, Patricia Meyer, 148

Talented heroine: aspiration and, 112-115, 140; conventional women and, 10-20; defined, 7-10; dilemma of talent of, 140, 141, 144; self-definition of, 39, 66-69, 110, 111; self-image and, 22-24, 46-47, 61; society and, 21-22, 61. *See also* names of individual heroines
"Task, The," 21, 22-23
Tave, Stuart, 119
Tennyson, Alfred, 5
Trudgill, Eric, 146

Tulliver, Maggie (heroine), 7, 8; aspirations of, 113, 114, 132, 136-138, 141, 142-143; compared to Dorothea Brooke, 56, 57, 59, 136; compared to Elizabeth Bennet, 86; compared to Jane Eyre, 86-87, 114; compared to Lucy Deane, 17, 18-19, 54; as lacking accomplishments, 9; self-definition of, 66, 68, 69, 81-89, 110, 137; self-image of, 21, 24, 39, 46-47, 53-61, 140; society and, 21-22, 101; as teacher, 103. *See also Mill on the Floss, The*

Victorian Ladies at Work, 145, 146
Victorian Wives, 145, 146
Vindication of the Rights of Woman, A, 5-6

Wives of England, 64
Wollstonecraft, Mary, 5-6
Women: duties of, 66-67; as governess, 100-102, 104, 111; marital expectations for, 119; nineteenth century expectations of, 64-65, 82, 85, 96-97, 98, 106, 152 n.23, 153-154 n.3, 154 n.6, 154 n.11; nineteenth century stereotypes of, 1-5, 8, 13; search for identity of, 63-64. *See also* names of individual heroines
Women and Marriage in Victorian Fiction, 148
Women of England, The, 66-67
Woodhouse, Emma (heroine), 7; aspirations of, 113, 114, 127-132, 141; compared to Dorothea Brooke, 91; compared to Elizabeth Bennet, 31, 37, 127, 128; compared to Isabella Knightley, 13-14; compared to Jane Eyre, 38-39, 44, 127; compared to Jane Fairfax, 14-15; compared to Maggie Tulliver, 81; as lacking accomplishments, 9; self-definition of, 66, 68, 73-80; self-image of, 21, 22, 31-38, 39-40, 140; society and, 101, 127-132, 141-142. *See also Emma* (novel)